Theater & Propaganda

Theater & Propaganda

GEORGE H. SZANTO

University of Texas Press Austin & London

Library of Congress Cataloging in Publication Data

Szanto, George H 1940–
 Theater and propaganda.

 Bibliography: p.
 Includes index.
 1. Theater in propaganda. 2. Drama—History and
criticism. I. Title.
 PN2049.S98 801′.952 77-8827
 ISBN 0-292-78020-6
Copyright © 1978 by the University of Texas Press

Printed in the United States of America

Chapter five was reprinted with minor revisions from
"Samuel Beckett: Dramatic Possibilities," *Massachusetts
Review* 25, no. 4 (Autumn 1974): 735–761. We are grateful
to the editor for permission to make use of this material.

FOR KIT

CONTENTS

PREFACE

Perhaps this study will be seen as a thing caught between two disciplines. For the social scientist interested in information theory and the ways by which information may be distorted into propaganda, the sections of the book dealing with certain plays and films may appear trivial: are there not more important forms of propaganda to examine? For the humanist interested in literary texts and their construction, including the history of their forms and their content, the sections discussing inherent and imposed methods of distorting information may seem an overstressed framework: why not get right down to texts, and so have time to examine a few more examples? Possibly it will be said: here is an essay caught between the analysis of propaganda and the examination of theater pieces.

It was not and is not my intention to have this study caught anywhere. In the Polemical Introduction I have attempted to define the shape of the book. In addition, I would like to suggest one guideline: that the reader bear in mind that this is a study of relationships that exist, beyond disciplines, in a world confronted daily by anyone who turns on a television set, who hears a report of a conversation, who oneself gossips—by anyone, that is, who obtains information through any narrative medium. *Theater and Propaganda* is a work resulting from the confrontation of my private interests in theater and my public interests in teaching, in exploring ideology, and in trying to understand why very many of us are, and have been for centuries, so strongly affected by depicted fictions. It is in this respect, I would suggest, that plays do embody primary problems for propaganda analysis.

Many of the ideas in this study grew out of practical and theoretical discussions with Milt Savage and Welton Jones, who, though they may each disapprove (differently) of my formulations, taught me a great deal about theater. And, while mentioning people who have contributed with their questions and ideas to that bit of clarity I might bring to theater and its relation to propaganda, I wish also to thank Robert Tucker for his encouragement, Donald Theall and Darko Suvin for their insights, and Sister Gertrude Gagnier for the privilege of peaceful study in the library of Notre Dame College, Manchester, N.H.

Special thanks go to the Academic Senate of the University of California, San Diego, for giving me a research grant which allowed me to begin this study, and to the graduate faculty of McGill University for a grant to bring it to its conclusion.

Theater & Propaganda

Chapter One

POLEMICAL INTRODUCTION

Audiences are comprised of persons who react both similarly and differently to the piece of theater they are watching. Whether the drama is presented live on the stage, cinematographically in the movie theater, or electronically on the home television screen, what is enjoyed by some may be despised by others. Often, the more explicit the message or ideological intention of a play, the stronger will be the applause or the disapproval. Among the negative reactions to ideologies expressed by a play, the phrase "Oh, that was nothing but a piece of propaganda" makes its periodic appearance. This kind of reaction is rarely based on analysis of the play or of the production. Rather, it is usually an individual's immediate and apparently commonsense response to the theater experience. Such an association or equation of the production to propaganda comes about after the viewer's reaction has been filtered through at least one intervening, most often not conscious, factor: that the play has presented a situation that was not and could not be real or true. So the process of rejection might be schematized:

$$\text{this production} = (\text{falsehood} =)$$
$$\text{propaganda} \rightarrow \text{rejection}$$

In the schema, the notion of propaganda has taken on the rather hazy meaning, "someone else's wrong opinion." Such a popular conception of propaganda can serve an audience member as an easy basis for dismissing the play and its intentions.

It does not take a highly self-conscious audience to

recognize, pragmatically, an incorrectness in depicted conversations or situations, the nature of which runs contrary to the usual juxtaposed circumstances of the audience's experience. A play which attempts to depict the beauties of religious security to an atheist, the simple pleasures of the tractor driver's postrevolutionary commune to the corporate capitalist, or the delights of cannibalism to the vegetarian, will usually fail to bridge the gap between its own ideology and that of the otherwise committed viewer. Instead, it will provoke his and her rejection of that given piece of theater, by way of the created association between supposed falsehood and such easily rejectable labels as "propaganda."

At the other extreme, the same piece of theater can be seen as a truthful depiction of reality, and so as a fine work of art, by audience members whose own experiences or even lives have run along patterns similar to those depicted by the play. The successful entrepreneur in the audience may well appreciate a theatrical depiction of the difficulties and glories of achieving business success, and a devout Christian can still enjoy the ideological as well as the aesthetic patterns of the late medieval *Everyman*. In the late 1950's Jack Gelber's much-appreciated nihilistic play, *The Connection*, struck a long-running chord of sympathy in his audience. This play already contained within itself the sympathetic reaction many viewers experienced; it depicted a series of circumstances often parallel to the structure of events in members of the audience's own existentially impotent and withdrawn lives (though metaphorically; the play used the world of junkies and pushers as its metaphor). Dialogue within the play verbalized audience reaction. The play presented a considerable number of moments or situations of utter impotence; in response to each of these, one of the characters would speak the melodramatic refrain, "That's the way it is, man, that's the way it really is." The refrain, a magical incantation of deficient but comforting truth, could be heard echoing in the audience and beyond. To a non- or anti-nihilist, the play was pure, obvious, and destructive propaganda.[1]

It becomes possible then to conceive of two extremes to a continuum: propaganda, the total falsehood, on the one hand; and on the other a totally valid depiction of reality, or truth. For some in an audience, one of these extremes might be translatable into an artwork. In an audience member's normal association with works of art it is, however, rare that the experience of a play or sense of a film will prove totally valid. At best, granting the experience great but incomplete validity is a far more likely reaction ("That was fine, I'd never seen it that way before, but it was slightly wrong here, and here"), since usually the experience of the artist which went into creating the play or picture is sufficiently different from one's own experience to allow for a critical gap. Or, historically, even if one's initial view of the artwork resulted in unmodified validation, often a later examination will result in more limited acceptance. It is even the case that one will precensor the chance for re-evaluation by avoiding a second look altogether, because one knows that the original reaction, while exceptionally strong, could not for one reason or another be repeated: "I was in just the right mood last Friday for X," we say; or, "I'm too old now to enjoy Q the way I did when it first appeared"; or, "Times have changed and so you can't take J seriously anymore." This does not mean that X or Q or J no longer give pleasure—merely, the new pleasure as experienced or assumed may be less than the previous, and so suffer by comparison. And of course, the opposite may also prove true. "I enjoyed *Gulliver's Travels* much more when I was twenty-five than I did when I was twelve (or eighteen) because I was old enough to understand its satire."

From such a range of legitimate responses it becomes possible to suggest that between the extremes of the continuum there are a vast number of positions, perhaps an innumerable quantity of them, each of which could concretely explain a relationship between an artwork's audience and the truth/propaganda value of that artwork.

There is an important problem implicit in this relationship, one which should be mentioned early: the nature of the connection between aesthetics and ideology, two of the important components of the created object or phenomenon. That is, to what in fact does an audience serve as movable, manipulable, malleable audience? Is it audience to the *values* of an artwork, to its ideology? Or is it audience to the phenomenon "artwork," a phenomenon which usually implies a series of aesthetic standards? I have argued elsewhere[2] that the aesthetic forms of an artwork are themselves functions of the work's ideology, that for any serious artist, and for any serious reader/ viewer, idea and experience find their form in the dialectical processes of creation (making; reading/viewing) at a specific moment in history. To suggest the opposite, that a preconceived formal arrangement should order the idea or the experience, implies an artificial relation between the content and its artistic shape, a relation that would deny a great deal of a work's validity, or truth-value, even before a consideration of either its form or its content has begun. So, in the subsequent pages I will examine primarily the relation between the audience and the values—the ideology—of certain works; the aesthetic matters will be considered only as issues of secondary importance.

Students and colleagues have asked why I speak of propaganda in relation to theater and not, perhaps more simply, directly of ideology. A number of distinctions between ideology and propaganda will, I hope, evolve from my arguments; one of these should best be explicit from the start. Propaganda is a specific form of activated ideology; that is, ideologies are manifested in various ways, and one such manifestation is the kind of propaganda the subsequent explorations will deal with. An ideology, on the other hand, is comprised of interconnected series of specific juxtapositions of values and beliefs. These values and beliefs may be drawn from the real world, or they may be an idealization of it—an idealization of the world as it was, or as it should be. Often these values and beliefs are hierarchical in their nature, and as a consequence an individual or a society expresses choices in terms of his or her or its ideology. Such choices, though certainly based on ideological presuppositions and themselves ideological in nature, are not themselves ideology. Rather, they are its signs, its manifestations. If propaganda is one form of activated ideology, then theatrical texts and their presentation are among the media within which ideological activity may be witnessed by audiences and by critical readers. A crass kind of temporal association between these elements can be depicted linearly in this way—

Ideology → Propaganda → Theaterpiece → Production → Audience

—recognizing that the elements themselves (like the relations between them) are dissimilar. The complex of historical dialectics among these elements is the subject of this study.

There are an exceptionally large number of possible relationships between the truth/propaganda value of the work and the numbers of audiences who will accept/reject the dramatic presentation. There is as well an inevitable change, or evolution, in the ideological nature of the reaction, over a period of time, on the part of any individual audience member. To a considerable extent, therefore, those who serve as audience to an artwork help control the work's meaning. In this sense, the meaning of an artwork changes as its audience changes. That the concrete work itself stays materially stable—the words of the soliloquy do not shift their places, the Giaconda smile remains reasonably intact—is of lesser consequence. Each new audience has new demands, new needs, that the artwork is called upon to answer. If the work has succeeded and continues to be of interest, it is retained in the repertoire or in the gallery, and remains what we call functioning art. When it ceases to work for an audience, it remains valuable for its place in dramatic or general aesthetic history (to which it may be relegated forever, or recalled if it is again needed).

And to the extent that an audience's perception of the artwork creates its importance, the audience displays its unique ideological needs through the demands it makes on an artwork. These vitalizing demands themselves evolve over a period of time, possibly bringing to the fore some previously rejected artifacts, while obscuring others. The choice and reapproval of works from dramatic or art history are themselves an expression of ideological need: Donne's highly individualistic poetry remains forgotten until Eliot's similar predilections tap a twentieth century consciousness by bringing him to the fore; Poe in Baudelaire's translation is more popular in France than is the original to its nineteenth century American audience; in the mid-1970's, Kipling is making a comeback; Aeschylus is rediscovered by the various renaissances after more than a millenium and a half of obscurity. Such literary exploitations of the past are not accidental; history and its artifacts are always most valuable to any daily present when they serve contemporary needs, when they give plausible answers to contemporary quandaries.

Though there are vast ranges of possible relations between all works of art and all audiences, the actual breadth of relations that exist at any given moment in history is somewhat less complex. For the purposes of this study I shall look explicitly at a reasonably limited period, at one form of artistic endeavor, and at one kind of relationship such an artwork can have with its audience. That is, I will attempt to deal only with the audience for modern western European theater, and that theater only at two points—at one of its beginnings, and at its mid-twentieth century moment—specifically to determine how such theater has functioned as a specific kind of propaganda, integration propaganda.

There are different kinds of propagandas, just as there are different ways in which propaganda can be made to function. The two which have had the most intimate effect on western societies and audiences are agitation propaganda and integration propaganda. Where agitation propaganda attempts to rouse its audience and society to active ends—patriotism, war, cheering for the home team—integration propaganda attempts to render its audience and society passive; its goal is for its audience to accept unquestioningly and uncomplainingly the social conundrums of the present and not challenge the authority of those who perpetuate the dominant and ongoing social institutions. The acceptance by an audience or society of a problematic situation with a "That's the way it is, man" reaction would be the highest aim of integration propaganda. It is the claim of the analysis of the next chapters that most popular western theater is the usually indirect (although occasionally directly planned) result of integration propaganda.

In addition, the analysis of drama will emphasize theater in electronically technological societies. Most contemporary theater, whether on stage, screen, radio, or television, is totally dependent on the technological discoveries of the past hundred years. The electronics of television and the cinematographics of film presentation are in fact the media for the greatest percentage of contemporary dramatic presentation. Even a play performed live on the stage is to a considerable extent a part of the technological society, its mechanical tools, and its rational consciousness.

But there is also specific importance in examining a phenomenon such as the Wakefield cycle of mystery plays. It is necessary to draw sharply the distinction between ideology and the technological implementation of ideology. Ideology has always existed, and so existed prior to electronic technology. At the time of the Wakefield plays, the dominant ideology called for a propaganda process very similar in intention and structure to contemporary propaganda processes. But, in large part because of the Wakefield Cycle's moment in the history of western technological development, the mechanics for implementing the desired propaganda processes were vastly different. The structured intention of propaganda, together with certain mechanics for its implementation, are central here. It will therefore be important to consider the significant degree to which contemporary technology serves as the mechanical and electronic extension for a presentation of integration propaganda by dominant classes within an ideology. That the specific content of the ideologies of the dominant classes has changed, and that the technology of the media for presentation of these ideologies has changed, is not primary for the purposes of this study. Essential rather is the (most often nonconscious) intentional similarity among all integration propagandas, their usually reactionary nature, and their services to the dominant social classes. I mean "nonconscious" in the sense discussed by Lucien Goldmann in *Le Dieu Caché*. The issue for Goldmann was not whether intentions are explicable by those who hold them, nor whether such intentions are hiding, preconsciously, at the corners of one's mind, nor whether the intentions have been profoundly repressed deep into the unconscious. Rather, such intentions are so intricately interwoven with a historically limited "common sense" that they have never been consciously dealt with by those who hold them. Such intentions always seem natural, logical, commonsensical, straightforward— they are based in assumptions which declare that things cannot be otherwise—that is, in historically nonconscious assumptions.

I will not attempt to examine in any total way the nature of different propagandas. However, chapter two will analyze the function of integration propagandas in and for a relatively stable society. Chapter three will explore the relationship between various forms of propaganda available to dramatic presentation. The next two chapters will look more closely at the manner by which integration propaganda is an inherent element in the Wakefield mystery plays and in the plays of Samuel Beckett. In addition, I shall use Beckett's work to present a double analysis—of the specific changes in relationship between the ideology of the artwork and the audience, and of the manner by which such changes can themselves be analyzed and subsequently grasped. The appendix attempts a preliminary and necessarily general model which a reader may find useful in breaking down and in overcoming the propagandistic intentions of an artwork, and it discusses the part theater can play in this sort of breakdown.

In addition, there is implicit throughout an intention to examine the vast distance between two generalizations, the idealizing and idealist "Art is the very opposite of propaganda," and the vulgar materialist "All art is propaganda." Though both these generalizations can at moments be seen to have validity, very quickly they obliterate any sense of the specific kinds of relations possible between art and propaganda. Such generalizations eschew analysis, and more: they most often prohibit it. Therefore, as a way into the wealth of possible associations between propaganda and art, I would like to mention a number of contextual considerations for this study. Through these it may be possible for the reader to agree with, or at least argue upon, a certain common ground, before (and then while) coping with the several parts of the argument. Perhaps in this way I can avoid confusion between the polemical and the formal elements in this essay.

The first consideration is the hypothesis, already suggested above, that the artwork has no intrinsic value. It may have great complexity, or delightful simplicity, or fine subtlety, or intelligent reasoning. But to an audience which finds subtlety foolish, reason a mystery, complexity intolerable, or simplicity naïve, such familiar adjectival description is not wrong so much as it is meaningless. A self-aggrandizing individualistic confessional poem serves little immediate purpose in a communal society; a baroque church ceiling would be grotesque and antipathetic to a naïve primitive. Taste, like aesthetics, will be considered a product of ideological education. Here are two portrayals of the relationship between a falcon and its reviewer: "I caught this morning morning's minion, king- / dom of daylight's dauphin, dapple-dawn-drawn Falcon, in his riding / Of the rolling level underneath him steady air . . ." and "This morning I saw a lovely falcon floating in the air and it made me very happy." Which is the "better"? The answer depends on the audience to the comment. One can find Hopkins' words bloated mouthfuls, or phrases of lilting beauty. One can find the paraphrase clean simple prose, or simply prosaic. The sources of judgments of quality lie outside the work. Beyond the work one can and will have ideological (and so aesthetic) priorities. In speaking of the quality of the artwork one speaks of a relationship between the work and those priorities. It makes little sense to say, "Such a work is good." It becomes important to ask, "Good for whom as audience, or what organization or class or sponsor, and why is the specific result of such appreciation a good thing?" The work of art which lasts in value for moderately large audiences over a long period of time may be more valuable, *because valuable to more persons in its audience*, than one which disappears quickly. Similarly, the extremely popular work which lasts briefly, the smash film or the blockbuster bestseller, may also be considered valuable because it is on some level exceptionally important for its audience.

Much work in both the historical and the synchronic sociology of audience taste must still be done before it becomes possible to speak of artistic quality in terms of audience values; but this may someday prove possible. Even when it is, however, such explanations will themselves be only part of a larger construct, no part of which will be able to claim for a specific work, "This piece of art is intrinsically good," and "This is intrinsically bad." It will only be possible to say that at point *A* in history an artwork affected certain parts of its audiences in one way, and at point *B* in another; and from, for example, a progressive ideological perspective the effect at point

B is better, or from a revisionist perspective far worse, or irrelevant. This rejection of the notion that a work has intrinsic value should not be read as a retreat to passive relativism. Rather, I will be arguing, implicitly and explicitly, that there is a perceivable historical, material, and dialectical relationship between the formally explicable nature of the artwork and various changing degrees of need in audiences for that form. All works of art have socially tangible and, to an increasing extent measurable, extrinsic value.

I shall attempt to avoid, as much as possible, such critical language as might obscure meaning. However, because some kinds of technical language can often act as a shorthand to explain concepts which would otherwise require dozens or hundreds of words, there are a number of terms which will have to appear. Two of the most central of these should be explicit beforehand; the others will, I hope, become clear in their context. Primary is the concept *institution*: by this I mean the product of a culture or of an economic or political society, a culture or society which has certain analyzed or at least analyzable requirements. An institution can be an intellectual and/or psychological phenomenon, such as linear thought; it can be a physical and/or concrete phenomenon, such as the Catholic Church. In addition, it can be the sum of a series of practices which allow concrete and psychic phenomena to interact, such as imperialism, or the golden rule. In all three cases, specific institutions are phenomena which serve specific ideological segments of societies. As such, institutions can be progressive or reactionary, flexible or adamant, long-term so as to appear eternal when one functions within them, or short-lived so as to seem vacuous when one sees them in a historical perspective. The phenomenon of dramatic production and the concept of intrinsic value in artworks are both institutions. And the producers of integration propaganda are usually institutionalized elements of the society.

Second is the concept of *hegemony*, a political notion extensively and intensively explored by Antonio Gramsci and recently employed in a cultural context by Raymond Williams. Williams explains hegemony in this way:

> ... hegemony supposes the existence of something which is truly total in society, ... which is lived at such a depth, which saturates the society to such an extent, and which, as Gramsci put it, even constitutes the limits of common sense for most people under its sway, that it corresponds to the reality of social experience. ... if ideology were merely the result of specific manipulation, of a kind of overt training, which might be simply ended or withdrawn, then the society would be very much easier to move and to change than in practice it has ever been or is. This notion of hegemony as deeply saturating the consciousness of a society seems to be fundamental. And hegemony has the advantage of other notions of totality, that it at the same time emphasizes the facts of domination.[3]

The concept of hegemony, extended and elaborated in the following chapters, will be helpful in an examination of the ways social and cultural circumstances set the limits on the kinds of art possible for a given society, as such a society is found to exist in man-made history.

My wish, beyond polemics, is twofold: to analyze the nature of integration propaganda so that it becomes visible to western readers for what it was and remains, a tool of the dominant class in any society; and to examine the manner by which unself-conscious propagandistic methods have saturated dramatic presentation. Perhaps if some of the more subtle forms of inhibitive and destructive propaganda can be examined in their several guises, it may begin to be possible to overcome both these and the human problems which such propaganda can conceal.

Chapter Two

INFORMATION, DISTORTION,

PROPAGANDA:

CONTROL FACTORS IN TECHNOLOGICAL

SOCIETIES

A discussion of the importance of propaganda within and between technological states calls for a consideration of the seminal work of Jacques Ellul. His analysis of the nature of propaganda in technological societies has expanded and restructured most western conceptions about the nature of information.[1]

All information has its context; information never exists in a vacuum. It is gathered, created, molded, edited, packaged, released, sent out from a specific source to a specific audience in order to achieve a specific end. There is no such phenomenon as "objective" information; this claim is Ellul's constant message. My preliminary purpose is to look at the processes by which information becomes distorted for and among a public, an audience which North Americans can recognize: themselves, we ourselves, as members of a specific technological society.

Consciously or not, all vested economic interests function primarily to keep themselves, their institutional progeny, and their value systems in a position of dominance and so of control. When I speak here of the propagandists, therefore, I do not mean a national or international cartel of information makers and controllers with regular transatlantic board meetings, operations outlets, and production staffs. I mean instead the social processes which collect, weigh, edit, reveal, and conceal information for the furtherance of a technological state and its values. So when using the term *propagandist* I will be momentarily anthropomorphizing these processes in order to bring some order to a very confusing and often too lightly examined phenomenon. In addition, the beginning of this examination will deal with propaganda of a generally literate sort. In subsequent analysis I will turn specifically to theater.

Literacy and Information

Ellul cites this formulation by Paul Rivet: "A person who cannot read a newspaper is not free" (p. 110). This part of freedom is, for Rivet, a person's complete, intellectual, conceptualizable and conceptualized comprehension of phenomena in linear, that is, literate, form. Ellul chides Rivet for requiring literacy as a precondition for human freedom.

Ellul fears the equation of high literacy with freedom. The person capable of reading, the person aware (because it has often been told him or her) that literacy will make one free, is the most easily propagandizable. Such a person has in fact already been propagandized into believing that reading will make, or has made, him or her free. The assumption that ability to read results in the probability of human freedom is based in a false cause/effect relationship. A supposedly value-free formal category, reading, is intended to lead to a reader's ability to engage in clear-sighted formal critique of content, in the world and in the reading matter, and so free the critic from his or her own unexamined value-structured thinking. The confusion results from an inadequate analysis of the content of what is read. That is, the mere ability to read can be and is used by the teacher of reading (the state, the school, the church, the instructor) to expound and validate certain kinds of information to the exclusion of other kinds of information. The classroom teacher may be—though usually such a one is not —aware of his or her role as a voice for partial, culturally determined information, the objectivity or at least value of which has been codified by the school board or by a reading list of essential texts.

In either case, there is nothing in the mere ability to read, even to read "critically," which guarantees a free and humanized reader. The very medium of print contains its own values within which the proponent of even "critical" reading is caught, since reading is the medium of consequential rather than simultaneous thought, analytical rather than dialectical reason. "Reading will make you free" is itself a piece of propaganda. Ellul writes:

> People used to think that learning to read evidenced human progress; they still celebrate the decline of illiteracy as a great victory; they condemn countries with a large proportion of illiterates; they think that reading is a road to freedom . . . They attribute authority and eminent value to the printed word, or conversely, reject it altogether. As these people do not possess enough knowledge to reflect and discern, they believe—or disbelieve—*in toto* what they read. And as such people, moreover, will select the easiest, not hardest, reading matter, they are precisely on the level at which the printed word can seize and convince them without opposition. They are perfectly adapted to propaganda. (Pp. 108–109)

It is such propaganda in its myriad forms which serves as the lubricant that allows a technological society's interlocking complexity[2] not merely to function smoothly, but to regenerate itself. When each human participant comes to see himself or herself as a well-oiled cog in, for example, "progress," then he or she has learned, often by reading, that a citizen's responsibility lies in the unchanging continuation of his or her assigned role. Thereby, too, the society can run with minimal friction. For the past four hundred years and until the early 1950's, the printed page was the primary medium for the dissemination of new information dealing with an individual citizen's part in helping a system work, and how best he or she could cope within it. While Ellul does not deny revolutionary functions to the history of, for example, the pamphlet or the broadsheet, he makes it clear that the western mind has been bound and limited by its literate skills. "The most obvious result of primary education in the nineteenth and twentieth century," he writes, "was to make the individual susceptible to super-propaganda" (p. 109).

Just as Ellul is opposed to Rivet's simplified view of the importance of literacy, his perspective also stands in opposition to the notion that literary linearity can be rejected in the cavalier manner championed by Marshall McLuhan, a notion which can stand some re-examination. McLuhan's work saw freedom as a phenomenon based in the total perception, in a non-Aristotelian acceptance, of information. McLuhan asked that information—each message received by the senses and translated in the mind—be accepted in the random order of its appearance. In addition, the individual's and/or the community's reaction to this information should also take place in nonlinear fashion. McLuhan described post-Renaissance western man as captive within a series of closed information systems in which the individual is the discrete unit and wherein most, perhaps all, human activity is dominated by the Cartesian *cogito*: self-consciousness is the prime value. Within the *cogito* all definitions for human relationship emanate from the individual in self-generated and active linear, rather than self/other, or interactive, fashion. Certainly McLuhan, with Ellul, pays at least passive homage to the monumental achievements attained within the long period of post-Renaissance individualism, to the remarkable technology that could free the world's people from drudg-

ery, starvation, and poverty. But both find it clear that
a time is at hand when linear reason, the closed cause/
effect relationship and at one time the mechanical basis
for a progressive technology, is no longer sufficient for
natural human survival. McLuhan's work served in the
preliminary process of negating his society's linear consciousnesses. He presented his audience with concepts
based in more communal, or at least in anti-individual,
perceptions of daily experience by rejecting the importance of the *medium* of print. He explained that a reader
can experience the printed line only individualistically.
In time his broad-based theories have come to appear
oversimplified, to a great extent only popularizing the
research, and analysis, of others, but in their own day
they imposed a vastly different primary category of
thought onto the attitudes of large numbers of people.

The difference between the work of McLuhan and
that of Ellul, in terms of their rejection of printed information as a potential liberator of the mind, lies in
this: McLuhan would turn to large-scale structureless-
ness in institutional and political life, accepting all information from all extension media as valid, and would
build from such information a communal, nonhierar-
chical utopia founded on the interrelated needs of his
world community. Ellul, on the other hand, recognizes
the impossibility, even as a working hypothesis, of such
a concept as "all information." All information has a
source and is therefore partial. Since most partial information is in existence to serve the ends of its producer
and/or its distributor, it serves propagandistic ends. For
Ellul the contradiction between information and objectivity cannot be resolved by additional information; if
resolution is to take place, it must be through the rational processes of the individual person. Negation for
Ellul does not grow from a change in social conditions;
negation is based in a dialectic of mind.

It is possible then to characterize three positions with
regard to the relationships among literacy, information, and the concept of freedom in a technological soci-

ety. Rivet, for our purposes, stands for the popular belief
that preliteracy implies captivity within a world so tiny
as not to allow civilized human intercourse. Only when
persons become literate can they become free, because
literacy will explode their tiny world and will let them
see an infinity of possibilities.

McLuhan suggests that preliterate men were free
(for McLuhan, preliteracy belongs primarily to pre-
Gutenberg time, and in a carefully restricted sense to
contemporary nonliterate peoples as well[3]), though free
only within their tiny community. The world outside
their community was not yet a factor. A lack of knowledge about the larger world was not important if that
larger world presented no threat, if it did not have to be
controlled. With literacy comes uncontrolled knowledge
of the outside world. Literate man is for McLuhan a captive of his linear intellect. Literate man has been taught,
by the very form of literacy, to utilize his linear intellect
in his attempt to control by domination that external
universe. But this attempt will be in vain. The universe
is far too large, visibly and invisibly too complex, for
any man with even a highly developed *cogito* to hold
rein upon it. With postliterate man, however, McLuhan
suggests, freedom is possible once again. Such a freedom
implies an avoidance of ideological contexts, together
with a society peopled by individuals who are capable of
reacting wholly to all stimuli. By *wholly* McLuhan
means: more than rationally/intellectually: "directly."
The literate rational intellect, used alone, stultifies; man
must exercise the intellect, but must also limit its domination by bringing to bear equally strong counterforces,
founded in a simultaneous and mosaic rather than in a
linear acceptance of information.

Ellul's work generally agrees with McLuhan's historical critique but is opposed to the prophetic model;
their theses run parallel, up to the point of postliteracy.
Preliterate persons are not yet psychically bound because all elements of their small worlds are open to
them. They are unpropagandizable. That is, they are

free from the domination of linear information.[4] The
literate person, on the other hand, is normally a captive
of the propaganda his or her reading gives access to. But
for Ellul, there is no such phenomenon as postliterate
man; whether not yet or not ever is not for him the
issue. Ellul recognizes only a higher level of literacy,
that in which reading, the transmission of information
through print, has been made subservient to the intellect. The intellect must force a critique of information
in order to demonstrate the manner in which the content of the information has been edited, overrepresented,
mythicized, miscontextualized—distorted into a message
necessary to serve, consciously or not, the goals desired
by the source of the information. The extent to which
the intellect itself has been structured by the very forces
which it must in turn "objectively" examine remains
in Ellul's work an unexamined contradiction; though
the distinctions Ellul makes between kinds of propaganda are exceptionally valuable, his lack of analysis of this
basic contradiction should be borne in mind throughout. I shall return, below, to the contradiction itself.

Ellul deals with distortion in several information media. I am stressing literacy here because reading has
been the primary mass distribution form from the days
of Gutenberg to the advent of television. Such reading
has dominated, and to a great extent still controls, the
manner in which most of the other media, certainly including nearly all postgothic theater, present information. Before considering the ideological dominance of
print over other media, however, it is necessary to examine the nature of distorted information and the manner by which it is made to serve, most recently, western
technological societies.

Kinds of Distortions

In the beginning I would like to avoid a discussion of
the divisions between conscious and nonconscious intent

in the creation of distortions. Information is transmitted, as a series of verbal and visual messages, through the initiating medium of a mind or minds, to another mind or minds. The initiating mind is limited by its ability to perceive and gather the content it is to transmit. Its information-gathering practices will be fragmentary. Consequently, even the clearest mind will be incapable of the objective presentation of material. The receiver of information, if aware of this limitation on the received information (the partiality of the material content), does not assume that the limitation can or will be overcome. Nor could the information's transmitter possibly transcend this limitation.

A distinction must be recognized here between an awareness of the partiality of information and the retreat of the subjectivist, the claim that everything is relative anyway so why bother even discussing an issue. Objectivity as a (nonachievable) form, and relative reductivity, are valuable in quasi opposition only when they lead to an awareness of the existence of limitations both in the tools for getting at information and in the kinds of information available. Such opposition can lead to the possibility of overcoming limitations dialectically; that is, under certain circumstances clarity of a sort can be attained by placing the (false) opposites, objectivity and relative reductionism, in juxtaposition, and then following the shifting perspective that results from negation by temporal progression. Those circumstances must at least result in the positing of new hypotheses along the way, hypotheses which are valuable because they can provide a common basis for critique, rejection, and so clarification.

Such institutions as national states that allow linear rational thought to exist publicly can convince themselves that they are open, democratic, objective, and analytical. Similarly, a person or an institution which transmits "all the available information," which presents "both sides of the issue," has assumed he, she, or it is functioning objectively, and would be indignant at the charge of acting as an extension of the institutions that disseminate integration propaganda. The distinction between conscious or nonconscious awareness of distortive message sending is therefore often not verifiable. Nor for the moment need it be. It need only be understood that a member of an institution makes propaganda out of information. Such a one uses information to serve the ends of the institution with which he or she identifies. The information minister of a democracy produces political ideology, the philosopher produces analysis, the public relations expert produces advertising; the overseer in a factory who produces simplified work rules, the Jesuit who produces theology: all are technicians in the production of propaganda.[5]

The propaganda produced is of two sorts, overt and covert—or as Ellul calls them, white and black propaganda. White propaganda is the visible kind, produced by the ministries and the public relations persons. Black propaganda is hidden, and the propagandee is unaware he is being subjected to influence. These two extreme forms are rarely used independently. Often, for example, white propaganda acts as a mask for black propaganda. Ellul explains: "One openly admits the existence of one kind of propaganda and of its organization, means and objectives, but all this is only a facade to capture the attention of individuals and neutralize their instinct to resist, while other individuals, behind the scenes, work on public opinion in a totally different direction, seeking to arouse very different reactions, utilizing even existing resistance to overt propaganda" (p. 16).

In addition, propaganda serves two primary purposes: agitation propaganda attempts to bring about change in a social circumstance; conversely, integration propaganda serves to bring a freeze to the social circumstance. Agitation propaganda is found in its highest forms (but not only) in a prerevolutionary-to-revolutionary state. It attempts to bring citizens to the proper point of radical awareness so that they can afterwards be moved to voluntary action. Ellul stresses this point: propaganda does not move people to action; to suggest as much oversimplifies the effect of propaganda. Instead, propaganda must be seen as a step or series of steps prerequisite to action, as the preparation of the minds of those who will later carry out the purpose of the propagandist. "Later" will come only after an event or a situation which has become intolerable according to newly learned perspectives triggers the action desired by the propagandist. Even the most simpleminded forms of agitation propaganda, certain kinds of mass advertising, function in this fashion. No woman will rush right out to buy a specific pack of cigarettes upon being told she's come a long way; but the image of herself as sophisticatedly fashionable is intended to prey on her mind sufficiently so that later, when she wants a cigarette, she will buy the proper brand.

In settled western society, integration propaganda is a much more familiar phenomenon than agitation propaganda. But its presence is so pervasive, its effect so permeating, that one becomes aware of its existence only with great difficulty. Integration propaganda suggests that all is well with the world, that one should accept one's society and participate passively within it. Most integration propaganda is covert. It must be constantly present if a technological society is to function smoothly. Integration propaganda is a long-term phenomenon, says Ellul, "a self-producing propaganda that seeks to obtain stable behaviour, to adapt the individual to his everyday life, to reshape his thoughts and behaviour in terms of the permanent social setting" (p. 75). If social revolution is permanent fluidity and change, successful integration propaganda is the key to the anti-revolutionary state.

Any hegemonically controlled liberal/conservative hegemony depends strongly on integration propaganda. Integration propaganda's purpose is preventative: to avoid unplanned change. Political and social stability is the key to the welfare of the reigning classes or factions of society, those who control the structures of relationships among the forces of production at such a society's economic base. A class-free democratic society, on the other hand, may well foster agitation propaganda in order to bring about a dialectic between revolution and permanence. Such a dialectic would be built of the constant opposition between any institution and the forces of its negation. Any other dialectic is incapable of retaining humanizing control over technological and informational development. But (loyal) opposition, when reduced to a static balancing force, with time becomes conservative and/or reactionary simply by retaining old institutional forms (premarital virginity, let us say, or patriotic military parades) and imposing them on evolved realities (new sexual mores, or a nation with decreased militaristic pride).

The dominant institutions of western middle-class societies fall more though not completely into this static liberal/conservative kind of balance. For example, in the mid-1970's, in most hegemonies, radical literature is readily available in a variety of underground (so-called for their own and their oppositions' propaganda purposes) newspapers and from a small number of presses. The liberal/conservative society calls radical literature "propaganda." Which it is; it serves the cause of agitation. In turn an underground press might call the mass media "instruments of propaganda." And they are, but of the other sort; they are media for the dissemination of white propaganda with integrative intentions. In the mid-1970's such an opposition results primarily in a lopsided but relatively stable balance. Freedom of the press serves the hegemony as an integration propaganda slogan, the meaning of which has five parts:

1. Our papers, the liberal/conservative press, are as honest as our honest reporters can make them.
2. We believe in the freedom of the press—therefore we allow any and all muckraking underground papers to function.

3. Their sensationalist reporting is nearly always a series of slanderous fictions.
4. In the arena of public information, virtually everyone accepts the word of the liberal/conservative press and rejects the radical tabloids.
5. Therefore our papers tell the truth and allow but reject (avoid) the slanderous fiction of the underground papers.

This example of circular but popularly adequate *cogito* reasoning is consistent with the network of preexistent structures, ideological and political as well as economic, which have formed the information acceptance/rejection continuum for the reader. The honesty of reportage within an ideology is always legitimate, yet also always limited, and so most often incapable of judging information beyond itself. That occasionally the validity of such external reportage should prove so overwhelming as to impose the acceptance of this information on both the liberal/conservative hegemony and its information media is only to substantiate the supposed flexibility of the hegemony, a flexibility learned in order to withstand more substantial, directly ideological challenge. And so it is said that absorbing Watergate tested the great basic strength of the United States—in fact, proved the very existence of that strength. True: from within the ideology of bourgeois corporate capitalism.

The larger dialectic between acceptance of information from within an ideology and acceptance of challenging information from without is, at certain (most) moments in history, frozen in favor of the dominant ideology. But history is a function of daily life, and people who live within daily situations constantly accept or reject the information they receive. To the extent that they reject information that seems invalid when compared to daily experience, they participate in the small dialectics of these daily lives, and so as well in the process of re-establishing the dynamics of the larger dialectic; that is, they participate in, by creating the basis for, historical change.

In western hegemonies, agitation propaganda when it occurs is clear because it stands out against a background of apparent permanence and coherence. Integration propaganda is hidden because it is part of the daily fare, a series of binding threads in the texture of the technological society.

Ellul examines the factors involved in creating and regenerating this texture. Such technique is a hypothetical form, supposedly value-free, the end of which is the attainment of a series of standardized methods for obtaining a pre-established goal (product, society, state of mind).[6] The corollary opposite of technique, which has to be posited here, would be another hypothetical form: total perception, total overview. Such an oppositional concept as total overview is helpful in establishing the intent of the propagandist. If total overview implies a broad though synchronically limited momentary conceptualization of the universe (ecology without history, one might say), then a propagandist is one who, consciously or unconsciously,

1. obscures the real overview;
2. presents a false overview;
3. maintains there is no overview;
4. attempts to create a valid overview from the bottom up, but goes wrong because his training is itself a product of propaganda,

in order to retain control for the hegemony and its technicians. The best propagandist would, and does, utilize a combination of these general categories, tailored to fit his or her material and audience.

Before searching out the specific intent of the propagandist it is helpful to look at the nature of his technique, of the theoretically possible distortions the propagandist can utilize in order to present his information. Although the emphasis here will be on integration propaganda and its relation to technological societies, some of the following sorts of media distortions are also the tools of the agitation propagandist and should be recognized as such.

Media distortions are of two discreet but usually interactive sorts, the formal and the material. Formal distortions can be classified as inherent medium distortion, format convention distortion, and selection distortion; material distortions can be divided among word, fact, and content distortions.[7]

Inherent medium distortions are a product of the choice of medium for the presentation of material. They are predetermined: a propagandist chooses his medium with its distortions in mind. Once selected, distortions are unavoidable within the framework of the medium chosen, since specific media limit their informational output in specific ways. The medium, that is, makes it impossible to avoid the distortion. Selection of the best medium for certain kinds of materials, together possibly with avoidance of other media, is the decision a propagandist must make. Hence a leader of state may make a major political statement to his countrymen on the radio because he has an excellent voice, and avoid television because he presents a bad visual image; or conversely, he may play constantly to the television cameras because his image conforms to such easily recognizable clichés as paternality, grace, or trustworthiness, and he will avoid making public statements unless the television press is present because he knows his words alone would sound vacuous. The medium itself creates the distortion by emphasizing one element of the subject. Radio news reporting can be more intense and central to an event or situation because it need not be slave to an image unobtainable after the unplanned event. Television reporting is best when it deals with such pre-planned events as political hearings, rocket launchings, and sports events. It is also a superior medium for presenting a regular diet of integration propaganda through the implicit value structures of regular shows, be they "trusted" regular commentary or comic and dramatic series.

The propagandist will weigh the strengths of various media. A newspaper, for example, with its primarily linear format, can cater to an audience's reason; its principle is to present one piece of information at a time, in an order presumably logical (though "logic" can be manipulated). Television, on the other hand, utilizes a simultaneity of presentation: both the image and the spoken word (and of course other sounds, but more of this later) contain their charged and controllable impact. Simultaneity on television can be used to reinforce information—to show that a president has an honest look about him when he speaks of "protective reaction raids"—or to undercut information by placing the image and the verbal presentation at odds with each other. Both reinforcement and undercutting can be elements of the situation itself or can be produced artificially by the broadcasting medium. In either case, the propagandist chooses carefully the medium or media which will best transmit his information.

When dealing with format convention distortions, the propagandist deals with the details of media morphology—layout, juxtaposition, and context. The conventional layout format of, for example, a newspaper can be varied to create emphases necessary for the propagandist's goal. A minor news story can be made into a screamer by giving it a banner headline. This device is used consistently by dailies which appear in a home edition and in a street edition—the home edition, delivered according to subscription, will often have one or two more (or longer) news stories on the front page than will the city edition sold on the newsstands, because the newsstand edition will head one of its less important stories with an eight-column headline as an advertisement for itself. The intention of the layout is to sell the paper rather than to give a perspective on the information.

In the same manner layout can distort information for less immediate though perhaps more basic economic ends. The ordering of information within a news story for purposes of emphasis, and as often for de-emphasis, must force a reader to re-evaluate the information in at least his own terms if it is to become useful to him in approaching a fuller understanding of the event described. Or similar information can serve as different message material by being placed within a variety of structures; when the structure takes a different shape, the information can be altered because of the shift in emphasis. Or, since juxtaposition of information is at least one important element in rational causality, the manipulation of informational sequence can create a variety of audience reactions, each with different ideological value.

The contextual distortions of format convention often serve a similar end. An important article which a periodical is, let us say, proud to point to in order to show its social concern may be cushioned by its place among whiskey and Steuben glass advertisements or by glossy color pictures promoting casual vacations in the Caribbean, scenes replete with yachts, sun, and girls in bikinis. Especially if the article's content is analytically depressing, juxtaposed suggestions of pleasure soften the blow and often distract the reader from the information itself. In television programming, context implies the relation of prime time (an economic phenomenon, as many of these issues are: how to render the product an integral, a *needed* part of the viewer's life) to the conventional expectations of the viewer. The nightly news integrates starvation and war into daily life; but if war, racial violence, or inflation news were to appear within the context of escapist entertainment, the juxtaposition could give the unprepared viewer a disagreeable shock. This would be a form of agitation propaganda; in a conservative hegemony, such an intrusion is rarely allowed into the prime watching time of the weary laboring (or unemployed and depressed) audience. The agitative connections between war and the alienation of daily work, or between unemployment and inflation, have no place in the hegemonic corporate technology. A democracy of the unaware cries out, silently, for integration propaganda to salve its weariness and discomfort. Not to be told that something is wrong is as good propagandistically as being told that all is really well.

The extreme kind of format convention distortion is selection distortion: the editor or programmer chooses whether a piece of information will be aired at all. Only a gloss of the selection-distortion issue is possible here. Selection allows a society's overall self-awareness, and so self-image, to avoid extremes of even vicarious experience. In a generally affluent capitalist technology there would be only a slight audience for information about rural socialism. On the other hand, liberal/conservative media audiences are only occasionally treated to explicit information parading the traditional American ideals of more, better, and stronger. For to do so would be blatant jingoism, overt propaganda, a presentation unacceptable to the doubting I'm-from-Missouri school of individualism and common sense which begins to smell a rat when a system protests its innocence too much or its virtues too loudly. At the same time, the media of the technological democracy do allow glimpses of alien systems—Nixon's trip to China gave U.S. viewers a good glance at the mainland, even at a few of the advantages China provides its people. But as Ellul would point out, such momentary glimpses do not perturb a great hegemonic technological system; instead they enhance the positive side of its image as a liberal/conservative state with an open forum, where all ideas are allowed to commingle in the marketplace—much more of an open society than, television viewers were constantly told, China itself, which would never allow its people to see portrayals of life within the United States.

Leaving aside the many possible responses to this charge, it is necessary to say only that such a hint of agitation propaganda (an extreme view of the media coverage of China, but for those hungry to get a sense of how a potentially sympathetic but unknown portion of the world functions, it was information to support sympathy for the mainland) gets lost in the sea of integration propaganda. It would have been much worse, for the hegemony, if American television had *not* covered Nixon's trip. For the integration propagandist, the less that is left to his audience's imagination the better. Freedom of speech, press, and imagination are still ideals. Nonetheless, the choice of silence is a possibility, the extreme of selection distortion. Saying nothing about an issue can be as basic a form of propaganda as a carefully detailed message. Just as the catatonic schizophrenic is communicating that he has no wish to communicate, so the silent propagandist knows that at certain moments it may be to his and his society's advantage to say nothing whatsoever. But in a liberal/conservative state, it is sometimes difficult to hide large actions and their immediate consequences.

This leads then to classification of the material bases of propaganda. Possibly it is also important here, along the way, to question the value of attaching labels to phenomena which are perhaps, to many readers, immediately recognizable. The intention of creating categories is not to obscure or to belabor the obvious; it is rather to provide a language for dealing with phenomena which not only surround but also confound and frustrate daily experience. Propaganda is at its best when it is presenting source-satisfying, source-concealing information. Integration propaganda attempts to obscure itself on all levels. Only by distinguishing between these levels and thereby demonstrating their presence is it possible to cope with its devious, often antihistorical and antisocial, functions. Resistance to classification, whether conscious or not, is common, and should be guarded against. Such resistance can be a sign of acquiescence to the propagandist. Labels for the categories of propaganda are, in the end, not important. Important is only that all kinds of propaganda be recognized so that they can be transcended, since even antihegemonic distinctions lose their value once the social conditions they attack are changed with time.

Word distortions come in various forms. Each serves a similar structural purpose: to confound the propagandee without allowing him or her to know he or she is being confounded. Word distortion may take these forms, to name a few: euphemism, implicational language, obscuring words, classificational clichés, generalization, cosmetic effects, association, or any or many of these in combination. In actual practice some of the categories will overlap. It might be difficult to separate out the cliché-which-classifies from a generalization, or a cosmetic effect from a euphemism. But again: dividing up the whole of an effect is essential in order to show how the component parts function both separately and interactively to achieve a unified result (image, point of view, partial comprehension). Word distortions support each other. A euphemism standing alone is valueless to the propagandist—it will be recognized immediately and laughed out of existence. Only when it is part of a tissue of distortions will it take its active and difficult-to-reject place both in the repertoire of the propagandist and within the consistent tone of messages the propagandee receives.

There are two sorts of factual distortion. First is the kind already discussed, the dominant presentation of partial though true information. Second is the presentation of false information. This second, the popular concept, views propaganda as nothing more or less than a series of lies, bold-faced and so impossible for any reasonable person to accept. The lie concept is itself first assimilated, then reproduced by the integration propagandist who, when speaking of propaganda to an unaware (propagandizable/propagandized) audience, identifies all propaganda with false information used as agitation propaganda. So propaganda has come to mean the opposite of "truth" to liberal/conservative citizens. In fact, the clever integration propagandist will only rarely use the falsehood form of propaganda, and then often as the straw man which he himself destroys. When actually utilizing the falsehood the propagandist will surround it completely with verifiable factual material so as to render the sources of the central lie indiscernible. To present a falsehood casually in a world overflowing with information is dangerous unless the basis for purely false information is completely hidden. So the classified document, the confidential file, the top-secret drawer, all can be the "sources" of false information, sources which can never be examined by those wishing to get at the basis for a piece of created and/or exploited "information." Such secrecy, however, is at least in principle anathema to liberal/conservative citizens who have been taught that in a free society a person is innocent till proven guilty, freedom leads to truth, and open inquiry is the basis of individual participation in good government.

It is furthermore rarely necessary for an integration propagandist in a liberal/conservative society to use the extremes of false information, since there are mountains of real information available. One can organize this real information in so large a variety of ways as to create whatever effect one desires without ever resorting to falsehood. To try an example: Angela Davis, once accused of being an accessory in the murder of a judge in a California courthouse, could have been presented by a series of media as a fiery teacher of philosophy who believed in the necessity for the universities to serve as the vanguard of social change. Or she could have been viewed (and was) as a disruptive black radical communist troublemaker who wanted to destroy existing institutions. Both these images would be correct. But both are partial, both are presented from a carefully drawn perspective and with a carefully measured and manipulative rhetoric. It would be difficult to believe, from the perspective of one position, that a spokesman for the other was talking about the same person. Yet both accounts of Davis are correct, in that they are both true; in

each case the information has been edited so that its
residual message serves its transmitter. The integration
propagandist adapts the idiom of the message to the
audience, then uses it to lead the audience to the ends
desired.
It is under the auspices of partial information too that
narrative distortion takes place. The media of print and
of broadcasting are both participants in the creation of
fiction, genres always labeled as such (a novel, a story,
a drama—narratives all), which nonetheless achieve
their validity by virtue of seeming *real*—lifelike, recognizable, immediate or mythic, contemporary or eternal,
relevant. Fictions themselves serve the needs of the integration propagandist. Much work has been done in analyzing, for example, the relation of the rise of the novel
to the development of western technology; these processes have proven to be related. It is important to note
here, before discussing this kind of material at length,
that the ideological form behind most fictions, whether
dramatic or fabulated, functions for the society that
reads or looks at the narrative artwork as, most often,
a specific kind of integration propaganda. Popular fictions that are valuable as integration propaganda depict
characters who are successful if and when they accept
or come to accept predominant social values and the social institutions these values create. Crime and espionage
fictions portray a challenged municipal or national social system asserting itself and show that for goodness
and decency to exist this system must remain the dominant social force. The western and the adventure story
explore the possibilities of individual search for a frontier, but the hero comes to a happy end only when he
reintegrates himself into the established society or creates its facsimile by taming the new land (by marrying
the girl, by settling down, by eliminating challenges to
civilization—e.g., savages and primitives; in short, by
accepting responsibility). When such integration does
not take place, the ending can never be what we have
come to call happy. The implication is strong that living

happily ever after should be the goal of every social
being. Such an implication is created and reproduced
by, and so has become an implicit part of, bourgeois integration propaganda.

Any series of combinations of these five distortive categories results in the largest and least explicatable distortion. The final product of the successful propagandist
is a totally self-consistent, easily acceptable message,
one which may however leave members of the audience
with the hint of unease. This is content distortion. It is
partly a combination of the previous forms of distortion;
but partly too the whole comes to be more than a total
juxtaposition of its parts. It creates a *total sense of consistent reality* which to the nonanalytic mind (itself the
desired product of content distortion) becomes the very
essence of realism. Therefore, because of its unified texture, a piece of content distortion can be seen as such
only from outside itself. The job of the clever integration propagandist is to present a piece of content distortion so completely within the idiom of his audience that
it seems as if no distortion is in fact taking place. Often
the necessary language for the analysis of a piece of content distortion will itself be integrated into the message
of the distortion.

A film such as *Easy Rider* provides a case in point.
The film depicts this message: that young men who reject institutionalized society cannot escape it and so will
be killed by the least of human elements in that society.
For its impact, the film chooses as its content the *form*
of a denial of society: that in order to build a critique it
is necessary first to reject, to negate, the implicit values
of the society under examination. The film, instead of
finally becoming this analysis and critique, ends by positing only impotence. In addition, for the two young
men it is too late to go back; "We blew it," says one,
speaking of a life they left behind, a life where they
were integral members of society, albeit of a subculture.
Both a return and a future are impossibilities. Total
despair, or death, are the two alternatives. The finished

product, the piece of overall content distortion, is a superb piece of integration propaganda. The film was a fabulous popular success: playing with fire, approaching the edge of the precipice, is exciting because it suggests, both to the protagonist and to the society, dangers which need never be experienced. It is possible that content distortion will produce a sense of minimal unease in its audience. But because the distortion is analyzed always in its own terms, such potential is disarmed beforehand by blaming it on the guilty pleasure one experiences from having played with matches, from having allowed oneself to be sympathetic to social outcasts.

Content distortion demands a meta-analysis, an analysis which transcends both the idiom and the ideology normally adequate for rational acceptance of information. Part of the intent of this section has been to create a language for an analysis which cannot for the moment be embraced by the propagandist. The language must make one ask what the general areas are that can be examined in order to discover the extent to which propaganda has sold technological societies and their citizens on the lack of alternatives to a static liberal/conservative corporate state. The next step must be an examination of the created myths which still support bourgeois capitalism as an ideological system, the myths which make the specific content of integration propaganda possible and necessary.

The Myth of Science and the Myth of History

Integration propaganda is most successful when it satisfies the collective wishes of its audience. In a technological society, the propaganda provides, up to a point, a satisfaction of needs; by virtue of being partial like the information it presents, the satisfaction remains inadequate. Religion, drugs, and alcohol have in the past functioned in a similar fashion: an impotent worldly religion—incapable of satisfying the needs of its congregants, valuable to them only because it has abstracted their needs into institutional ritual, preaching that suppression in this life is dissolved in the next—is similar in structure and effect to drink and to drugs, which deaden the oppression of daily reality. All these function as salves to the propagandee; such salves may seem to satisfy needs previously created by the same social powers that then administer the opiate.

The process would be as circular as it sounds were it not for the temporal element: integration propaganda usually *follows* the needs and difficulties created by the hegemonic institutions. Integration propaganda provides its hegemony with unique control over the needs the dominant class has created in the society, partially by falsely satisfying those needs and partially by creating new needs. These needs will then be inadequately satisfied later on and can, according to virtually all information available, be satisfied only by the unified political state. The citizen of the technology, alienated or alienatable, must be convinced he or she will come to be part of this whole; only then will he or she fully support the state. Integration propaganda, like religion and drugs and alcohol, creates a sense of false unity. Such a unity is draining, deadening to the search for more basic solutions to human needs, because it provides a belief that the best in life has already been achieved. If a citizenry can be brought to believe this goal has been reached, then the desire for additional analysis, for negation, and for subsequent action has been destroyed, at least for the moment.

Most often the alienated citizen does not reject, indeed he or she comes to solicit, integration propaganda itself. In the daily milieu only integration propaganda (drink and drugs, religion, and other false information may be its content) will satisfy those appetites created in him and her by their liberal/conservative society. A politician's vacuous words about freedom and democracy and the individual's right to self-determination in every issue that affects him will function as supportive integration

propaganda which can be quoted by the citizen who is too
weary or too busy looking for a job to analyze the action
of that politician. The words are usually salve not to deep
wounds but to an itch which the citizen himself does not
really want to have to scratch either. There is both a
mostly unconscious fear that the itch is caused by a serious disease, and a sense that it is not pleasant to scratch.
Nonetheless, in a society where only the façade is democratic, the salve of integration propaganda must be ad-
ministered continuously or else the citizen will begin to
scratch when he starts to doubt a consistency between
the politician's and the hegemony's actions, and the civic
ideals the citizen has learned in school.

Similarly, integration propaganda caters to more private needs in the form of advertising: the accountant
knows he has within him the potential to be a rugged
outdoorsman if only he were transferred to a different
part of the country; the housewife who has come a long
way knows she too could be sophisticated if only she
were in the proper circumstances. Though these needs
are only of a secondary reality, the attempt to satisfy
them often comes into being as a tertiary reality; if he
and she smoke the proper brand of cigarettes, or use the
proper toothpaste or deodorant, they will be transported
closer to their real selves. Whatever need smoking answers, the least part of it is to make one appear rugged
or sophisticated. Nonetheless, the image as advertised
fulfillment of the need is accepted by a nonanalytic,
heavily propagandized audience as a real fulfillment,
and is desired as such.

Both the hegemony and the cigarette company, by
their corporate actions and on the surface through their
public relations services, utilize integration propaganda
for similar structural ends. Their success in this process
is based on the myths which are deeply imbedded within
the images both are creating. Ellul sees the two great
myths of western man as the myth of Science and the
myth of History. Myths of society, says Ellul, do not be-
long just to individuals or to specific groups, but are

"shared by all individuals in a society including men of opposite political inclinations and class loyalties" (p. 39). Science and History are the ideal hypothetical forms which, as oppositions, serve society best when they function in dialetical interaction. The myth of Science implies that all (of reality, of truth, of information, of objectivity) is present now, and only remains to be uncovered. The myth of Science is pragmatic and empirical. The myth of History implies that everything exists only in potential form, that everything must be worked out. Its method is dialectical. Science stands for the growth of knowledge; History stands for progress. The working goal of both is human improvement. But implicit in the myth of Science is the concept that the absolute in human improvement can be achieved, the utopia can be built; the myth of History suggests that so long as man is based in a material universe his condition will continue to change and the concept of improvement must be modified and developed for each new generation.

While Ellul's oppositions are valuable for this analysis, they are not, as he implies, value-free. The extent to which these myths are indeed shared by all individuals in a society is more limited than he suggests. The Marxist, for example, could not believe in the myth of Science as a basis for improvement in daily human existence, since Marxism functions according to the belief that present and future history is made not by institutions improving themselves within middle-class ideologies but by individuals working within collectives to create a classless society. On the other hand, the commonsense empiricist has seen from observation over a period of time that the mere passage of history does not change the basic realities he or she comes ever closer to describing. To say that my own perspective in the subsequent examination is based primarily in the myth of History is important only to the extent that the reader should know ahead of time the ideological basis for my attempt to integrate the myth of Science into the myth of History and so provide an additional mechanism for seeing and therefore overcoming various forms of integration propaganda, both those described here in this general discussion and later those found in specific kinds of theater. It is also important to know that Ellul rejects the reality of the myth of History, though he fully acknowledges its force in the minds of certain citizens of technologically advanced societies.[8]

Ellul goes on to explain that both these myths provide a base, though differently, for the secondary myths specifically pertinent to technological man: the myths of Work, Happiness, Youth, the Nation, and the Hero.[9] The integration propagandist could use both basic myths by enclosing them within the idioms of the secondary myths. In actual practice the propagandist for the liberal/conservative hegemony uses primarily the myth of Science. Utilization to any great extent of the myth of History could undermine his prime intention, that being to render his audience passive and satisfied, since the myth of History views all situations as open and changeable.

It is important to see the forms the five secondary myths take for Ellul, within the contexts of Science and History. By virtue of the values technological man has come to see as normal, the interpretation of the five myths from the point of view of Science will appear to him natural, while from the point of view of History they may appear startlingly, perhaps revolutionarily, pleasant —too good to be true, empirical positivistic man might say with a sad smile.

The myth of Work says that man must work in order to produce, in order to create an improved life for himself, for his family, for his society. The product can be a wheel, a mainspring, a new fertilization process, a new analysis, a better mousetrap. Both the myth of Science and the myth of History would subscribe, in general, to a need for improvement. They differ, however, in the method for achieving that product. According to the myth of Science the single most important element is the product itself; if it improves man's lot, the best way

of creating it is the fastest and the cheapest. The contradiction—that in making a cheaper nonbreakable mainspring the labor strength and value of the very human
beings for whom this product is supposedly being made
are drained from them forever—is unimportant. One of
the advantages of the myth of Science, as itself a piece
of integration propaganda, is that it can and most often
successfully does explain value in terms of product. By
ignoring the value of labor, it hides the whole question
of profit from examination by the workers who actually
manufacture the product. The difference between wages
and expenses, and the price the corporation receives for
the product, called by Marx the surplus value, must be
obliterated by the propagandist. At his best the propagandist can transform a production industry into a service industry: "Made better to serve you better." "Progress
is our most important product."

The assembly line worker who commits the same act
hundreds of times a day, having no sense of his function
in the finished product, is the extreme of this kind of
alienation. He is not different from the scientist whose
devoted experiments at the far reaches of knowledge
make it impossible for him to function as a member of
society. In his effort to fight such alienation, the propagandist exposes both assembly liner and scientist (and
not all that differently) time after time to information
which explains that the work they are doing is essential
to the well-being of the state or the community, that the
state is aware of each of them individually and appre-
ciates each. Nor need they be concerned about the use of
the product they have helped create. The biologist's work
can be turned into germ warfare content; the assembly
liner can help to assemble rocket guidance systems. So
long as they each believe their own participation in the
process is pure research, or is only a job, or they can remain ignorant of the nature of the final product, then the
task at hand can be made to appear value-free. In addition, if these workers are told that they are appreciated
by the technological society for which they are willingly

struggling, and they accept this blandishment, then the propagandist has succeeded. The contradiction—that as they work toward their personal improvement, promotion, recognition, praise, higher pay, and security, they create products for the potential destruction of others, and that they themselves are willing to accept such immediately visible rewards by giving up control over the use of their products—this is ignored. For a worker to demand as a right the control over at least a larger part of his finished product may seem trivial. But such a demand is a step toward eliminating the distance between the worker, his relation to other workers, and their part in the product they create. It moves the maker closer to participation in the myth of History in that it begins to suggest the possibility of human control over history, and the place of human beings in the production of history. That is, when the individual accepts responsibility for, and remains in contact with, the product he creates and its effects on the users, he has taken one step toward becoming aware of the function of these materials in the history of his time. Not a revolutionary step, to be sure, but the first of many necessary steps toward total social change. Such awareness may lead to the beginnings of his control over the future.

It is the function of the propagandist to thwart this process toward awareness and social self-control at every step. Since the function of the technology is to perpetuate itself, the individual or group must not be allowed to control any part of a hegemony's production or any of its economic powerbase. But should he or she gain any control at all, another branch of the propaganda corps must render him passive, satisfied, and unwilling to function as a member of a group with ends beyond those of corporate production. Here the liberal press, for example, becomes a visible factor in the integration propaganda establishment. For a corporation to allow partial control to its workers of the manufacturing process could lead to a momentary balance of control between the corporation and the workers. Such a balance might be

seen as desirable by a liberal press and consistent with
its ideology. But liberalism is founded in the myth of
Science. Often, therefore, the liberal press itself is not
aware that by demanding a retention of won but quickly
outworn conditions, it soon advocates a series of conservative conditions. Or to put it another way, when liberal
ideology thinks it freezes the superstructure at what looks
at one moment like an even balance, the corporate representative, after a short period of time (e.g., made history)
unbeknown to the liberal balancer, quickly reasserts
control over the economic base. Things do not remain
the same. To win a fair wage is valuable only when in-
duced inflation does not undercut it. Union control won
in the thirties and institutionalized in the forties had
become, in the sixties, often destructive to others making
reasonable wage demands because the awakened and
threatened union's position forced its complete identification with the hegemony. During the fifties, for a left-
liberal to criticize newly visible reactionary trends within trade unionism was no different, in the eyes of the
union establishment, from the red baiting of twenty
years earlier. And it was the job of the integration propagandist to let the potential critic know the great extent
to which his arguments would be deemed rightist by his
liberal colleagues. The fifties' propagandist succeeded.
Not till the late sixties did it become clear to a popular
consciousness that most big unions were inextricable
elements of the hegemonic bourgeois state.

The extent to which the taking of partial control of a
production process is successful, as seen from the perspective of the myth of History, is the extent to which it
is used as a basis for additional political and social struggle. To see participation in production control as a final
goal, as the establishment of an unchanging balance, is
to freeze an achievement in time, to let it be negated as
time passes, and to allow the reassertion of institutional
control by the hegemonic state—*because the hegemony
is aware*, sometimes consciously but much more often
not, *of the reality of the myth of History*. To retain con-

trol it must keep this reality entirely hidden from the citizenry, veiled beneath a myth of Science raised to its highest power; and this again is the job of the integration propagandist.

A myth becomes valuable when it is central to, and can be validated by, one's experience; and so it becomes central also in the description of a series of temporally circumscribed social phenomena. For a middle-class state, the myth of Work therefore occupies the most important position among the secondary myths. At earlier times in history, different myths would have been predominant. Those still important to bourgeois ideology—for pragmatic rather than sentimental reasons (except when sentiment can be made to serve pragmatic ends)—are residues of earlier systems and states,[10] residues which may be baffling to the integration propagandist but which he ignores to his great peril. The contrapuntal myths of Happiness and of Youth, for example, remain as important fragments of an otherwise surpassed two-hundred-year-old romanticism. Happiness is the passive romantic myth, Youth the active romantic myth. Both are myths of the individual, although in its more abstract form the myth of Youth can be expanded to serve the society as a whole, at which point it becomes linked with the myth of the Nation, the making of which marks the first modern attempt to create a communal ideology out of geographical limitations. The integration propagandist uses these secondary myths in relation to each other. Together they comprise the texture of their society's value structure; the utilization of any one will affect the condition of the others. "It is remarkable," says Ellul, "how the various presuppositions and aspects of myths complement each other, support each other, mutually defend each other" (p. 40).

The myth of Happiness, the achievement of a satisfaction of human needs, also changes when viewed according to the myth of Science or according to the myth of History. The myth of Science provides answers which can satisfy for the moment and must then be supported

by propaganda in order to convince the citizen that his
momentary satisfaction is a lasting one. For example, a
Raymond Chandler heroine, unconsciously attuned to
the myth's defects, says, "I always find what I want. But
when I find it, I don't want it anymore."[11] Satisfactions
founded entirely on the myth of Science are artificially
imposed, and so fail to meet nonmaterial ends.

Though it is much more difficult to realize Happiness
dialectically, the possibilities of this process were already
implicit in the romantic notion of Happiness. Hegel
claimed the greatest happiness to be found was in the
historical progression toward the Ideal; Goethe depicted
the happiness of Helen and Faust at its greatest heights
in their striving to bring their passion to perfection. The
romantic notion of Happiness is inseparable from dialectical development, motion, and change. For a bourgeois
hegemony such development, in the negation and the
subsequent creation it implies, is dangerous, all the more
so when Happiness transfers its progressive content from
an ideal psychic personal base to an external social material base. Over the years, therefore, the propagandist
has had to separate the myth of Happiness from a historical construct.

Although the myth of Happiness implies a desire for
security and comfort (Science), or resolution and synthesis (History), it can nonetheless live side by side with
the myth of Youth: exploration and discovery, potential,
the future, risk for great reward. Psychologically the
two myths do constant creative battle within each person; for European romantic man of two hundred years
ago, this combat was the highest form of progressive individualism. Its tradition remains. In the 1950's it provided a yearned-for retreat from technological alienation. And so the propagandist may use this conflict to
draw attention away from a serious shift of perspective
within the myth of Work. A form of this distraction lay
at the bottom of, as examples, the beat movement, the
popularity of the works of Albert Camus, the rediscovery
of Franz Kafka.[12] Or the propagandist may use it as a

rebuttal to the Historical view of the myth of Work: people are only happy when they come to terms with themselves, with their goals, with their desires. But in a discussion of the myth of Work, this kind of rhetoric soon begs the question: it allows the propagandist to dismiss all threats coming from outside his consistent system, breastbeating his relevance as he goes.

The ends which the myths of Happiness and of Youth can serve are as broad as the imagination of the propagandist is fertile and his goals are pervasive, from a man's home being his castle to *Time Magazine* apotheosizing Youth as its Man of the Year to everybody having his say in court, and beyond. The discomfort and/or the glory of young men refusing to fight in Vietnam could be seen as the great American Rorschach test ferreting out the dominant secondary myth: Horror at sending off the flower of American youth to war and death; Dismay at the softness of the generation of the future; Relief or Disgust that a middle-class education keeps one from becoming cannon fodder. For the integration propagandist, the more interpretations the better. As long as all argument takes place within the larger myth of Science, any tempest is teapot in size and controllable by that relieving dogma, "In a democracy we allow such discussions to take place." Or more correctly (and avoiding the implicit double negative): "In a bourgeois technology the myth of History must be kept invisible from the citizenry."

The myth of the Nation is a creation not possible without the myth of Science. Nationalism in its nineteenth century form was an attempt to establish the extremes of possibility so that an individual mind could cope within clearly defined physical limitations. When there are no visible or visualizable horizons, the mind and one's loyalty boggle at the thought of having to cope with daily difficulties standing between oneself and one's mediated goals. The largest limitation deemed workable in a Europe where communication was exploding in perspective was one determined, usually, by language groups, and the nation was created as the largest area within which a person need function. Ideally a nation would unite all people of one kind. In practice a nation became a form which arbitrarily enclosed groups with contradictory class and so social and ideological interests, and separated units within its borders from external but organically related groups. From the perspective of the myth of History, the notion that all people of one kind could be united within national boundaries is at best naïve and, more importantly, destructive to otherwise historically developed class relationships among people and among nations. Nonetheless, because some forms of horizontal limitations are essential, especially to bourgeois men and women, the nation persists, primarily for economic reasons, reasons essential to the continuation and furtherance of the corporate state.

The propagandist's success here arises from his ability to exploit tradition and sentiment (the myth of Happiness' dominance within the myth of Science: security, the good old days) in support of the Nation. Sloganeering is the easiest form of nationalism—"My country, right or wrong"; "America, love it or leave it." But it is far more invidious and nationalistically successful to call U.S. intervention in Viet Nam a mistake, suggesting it was only momentary deviance which let this country step from the path of righteousness; the integration propagandist can use even the national self-apology as a guard against any serious examination of the state's economic interests, within and without its boundaries. The myth of the Nation protects the national economy, in fact makes a reality out of the "national economy" concept which would be meaningless without the myth of the Nation.

The myth of the Nation, as it existed two hundred years ago, contained as a tenet the attempt to re-create communal boundaries within which a group of individuals could function for *mutual* interest. In the late twentieth century, the nation, like the city, is failing as a geographic unit to provide economic possibility and so psychic space for people to live in. There is a basic reason for this failure: the extent to which the Nation is in reality comprised of individuals who function successfully according to principles of *economic self*-interest rather than for mutual popular interest is becoming popularly visible. The contradictions within a state defined primarily by systems of competition allow the national state to function only so long as expansion, within the state, by competing forces, remains a possibility.[13] Once all internal room for expansion has been utilized, the state serves only as a constraint to competition. A larger form must be found. Historically, this was the role of imperialism. In practical terms the international conglomerate has done this by itself becoming a state, with loyalties only to itself and all its rules self-made. Internationalism of this sort must not become visible to the general citizenry, of course. Just as nationalism satisfied a need for individual horizons, it also obscured the citizen's view of the seat of real power. If it is extremely difficult even to see, to visualize, to abstract out the boundaries of the hegemonic national or international state, the state's control over its many citizens becomes relatively simple. Self-engendered plans for its future may continue undisturbed.

The last of the secondary myths Ellul mentions is that of the Hero. The Hero is a holdover from an earlier moment in European history, but one which gained importance with expansionism. This image is especially important on the American continent as an easily recurring archetype within a frontier context. The traditional western Hero myth is found in self-enclosed communal societies which have reached a point of decadence. When a traditional society has become inbred, a condition often symptomized by the society's unavoidable impotence as it is held under the sway of inexplicable powers, it can be and often was brought back to vitality by the stranger/ hero from the outside. Robin Hood the outlaw helps the poor against villainous tyrants; Beowulf comes from across the sea to save Hrothgar's people from Grendel;

Siegfried arrives from afar to win Brunhilde for Gunther
in a marriage which will guarantee the continuation of
the Burgundian line; Christ is sent from God to save the
Jews; where all others have failed, Kissinger flies by
night to bring U.S. face-saving withdrawal to Southeast
Asia; and the Lone Ranger comes from over the hill to
rescue the settlers. These are satisfying individualistic
mythomorphic patterns. Sometimes the hero removes an
impasse, which allows the community to function normally again; then he departs (who was that masked
man?). Other times the individual himself remains,
marries into the society and infuses it, materially, sym-
bolically, and/or literally, for future generations through
his children, with a new strength to continue. The two
forms of vital infusion are opposite sides of the same coin.
Either image is an adequate tool for the integration
propagandist; he asks for nothing more than that the
belief remain that one day the white knight will appear
and save the society of whatever ills threaten it.

The propagandist will usually admit that the society
is not perfect. But he will claim it is perfectable, a priori
within the myth of Science, and the shining knight,
through individual action, can save or improve or ameli-
orate or cleanse the society, and bring it closer to perfection. The propagandist nurtures the myth of the Hero
because he knows it is impotent in fact but powerful in
image—he knows that *the individual alone can never
alter the economic base of the capitalist state.* The propagandist takes the possible reality of the Hero—the one
who saves and represents, interactively, the group as a
whole—reduces the reality to an image, and then places
the image above the group. For the Hero to remain an
integral element of the group cannot be allowed by the
propagandist—a popular Hero is beyond the control of
the hegemony. Popular contact with the Hero humanizes
his or her image, weakens its effect as a tool of the hegemony. To weaken the image destroys the Hero's anesthetizing effect.

On the other hand, a Hero organically united with his

group, functioning according to their real daily material needs, is the shape the myth takes within the context of the myth of History. This Hero progresses with the group, leaving it only to attain the historical perspective needed by the group, returning to it constantly. This form of Hero the capitalist hegemony's propagandist will not allow because the Hero would begin to function according to the needs of the citizenry rather than according to the goals of the power structure. In addition, in a group as fragmented as that created by the liberal/conservative state, departure from and return to the immediate society becomes impossible. A rift will always be imposed, by individualistic ideology (a person's worth: greater for some than for others), between membership and leadership; the Hero must make a choice between roles. If one remains the Hero, even if one's original intents were consistent with the myth of History, one will most often be made into a Hero within the myth of Science by the propagandist who controls the image.

The Hero has been important on the American continent in a revitalized form, that of the outsider on the frontiers of physical existence, the self-sufficient person, most often an adult male who functions, successfully, according to the image created by the capitalist propagandist. In this respect the Hero is closely allied with the myth of the Nation because he implies the constant possibility of finding a new frontier in which the problems of an inadequate society can in theory be left behind. Frontier practice can seem to make anything possible. And he is even more closely allied with the myth of Youth in its social construct, in that the whole of the future is open to the man and to the land; the fruits of the exploitable future need only be grasped. In this respect the most "satisfactory" westerns and near-westerns usually end with the hero marrying the girl and settling down with her to expand her Daddy's ranchlands; the problems left over from civilization are rarely if ever discussed. Only the *establishment* of civilization is important. This is completely consistent with the integration propagandist's intentions: the Hero is a worthwhile figure until he has done his job (saved the girl from the savages, driven off the outlaws), a job which accepts bourgeois ideology, which never challenges this larger system. Once completed, the Hero becomes part of that system. His problems thereafter are too drab for analysis, implies the propagandist; they are problems like everyone has. Their serious analysis is unnecessary. The underlying implication: daily problems of living are totally natural, unworthy of collective analysis.

The propagandist brings the Hero, and much more often, heroic tendencies, under the sway of the hegemony. The Hero is valuable to the hegemony only when he is controlled by the state—created by it, and/or brought under its sway. Otherwise the Hero is dangerous and must be depicted as such. Hence the large number of black American leaders who in the sixties were depicted and branded as public enemies in criminal terms. Hence also another phenomenon, both literary and social, the easy label for which, in late-capitalist critical language, is "antihero." If the Hero is the man from the outside who enters the society to restore it to its greatness, the twentieth century antihero is the man pushed out of his society by the strains of liberal/conservative possibilities in life. He denies the value of the myth of the Hero only by the label of his name; otherwise he bears little resemblance to the Hero. But because the Hero is as an image still valuable to the hegemony, the propagandist gains double credit by branding the man who cannot live within the normal confines of the state and suffers outside it an antihero, someone in opposition to the Hero of the myth of Science, hence someone opposed to the values of the liberal/conservative state. The negative label makes the reject, according to the repressive morality of the hegemony, a bad example of humankind.

The myths of Happiness, Youth, the Nation, and the Hero are holdovers from moments in the past when they were dominant social forces. They are utilized by the propagandist, when necessary, along with the more contemporary myth of Work. I suspect the dominant functional myth for the upcoming era, a time period about which one can necessarily remain only vague, will be something like a mythomorph of Synthesis. Within it, the attempt to overcome the contradictions among the varied (because grown from different structures) needs of humanity considered as a whole, and interactive society, would be the primary, the predominant goal. From the perspective of the myth of Science, Synthesis would call for a bringing to human consciousness those phenomena, methods, processes, and technologies for attaining large-scale elimination of poverty, disease, starvation, and ignorance already available to some nations or other subgroups, with emphasis on a unification of knowledge rather than a stress on pushing forward the frontiers of knowledge. Of course, such synthesizing processes bring the myth of Science itself very close to the potentials implicit in the myth of History. From the perspective of the myth of History, Synthesis would be a process dialectical in nature—the creation of new resolutions, in theory and actuality, between phenomena and/or quanta of knowledge which had before stood in contradiction, or in mutually exclusive spheres. The myth of History would create, out of the secondary myth of Synthesis, a unified economic, social, and intellectual frontier.

Synthesis, from the perspective of both Science and History, already touches most forms of human experience. The mythomorph of Synthesis is on the way to replace completely the myth of Work, an increasingly abstract phenomenon as technology supersedes work with leisure, just as the myth of Work replaced the myths of Youth and Happiness as motivators of individualistic value systems. If the descriptions of the Science and History perspectives of the myth of Synthesis sound like the description of the primary myths of Science and History themselves, the coincidence is intended; there may well no longer be a need to experience these mythomorphic forms through secondary myths. Human improvement will be viewable—directly, in this emergent era—as a dialectic between the growth of scientific knowledge and human progress through the constant reconceptualization of a reality which improves, partly in planned ways, with the passing of time. But we are not yet at a time when the information media are prepared to propagate such abstract ritual phenomena as Ellul's primary myths. For the propagandist the primary myths are in themselves useless because they could speak to only the tiniest of audiences. For the hegemony they are potentially dangerous because their open discussion would potentially, if it became widespread, bring about the most basic changes in the liberal/conservative state—first, rendering it far more egalitarian, and second, opening it to evolutionary rather than to decreed progress. The first step in creating a new mode of life is to realize it as a possible, though not necessarily allowable, alternative to the present.

Ellul suggests, constantly though implicitly, that the ideal society would use both primary myths in order to satisfy the human needs of passivity and of progress. In this respect he is close to (despite his rejection of) Hegel, who, in Ellul's terms, describes the manner by which the myth of History achieves the ultimate goal, with the final synthesis possible only in God. The concept of God is quantitatively similar to Ellul's Christian understanding of the ideal society, appropriate enough for the sincere Christian Ellul. Yet at the same time his Christianity makes Ellul strongly pessimistic, and thereby very conservative. By taking the limits of description rather than the analysis of critique as his domain, Ellul refuses to engage in a negation of the system he portrays. His positivistic intellect, combined with his passive role as a social critic when he has so much of the content of his subject at hand, are completely consistent with the Christianity of an era limited by the myth of Science. Passive and moral Christianity is completely consistent with a liberal/conservative society. Selfless service to the contemporary community, refusal to hurt one's literal neighbor, acceptance of God as the final synthesis, these are as much a part of Ellul's moral world as they were part of Balzac's. But for Ellul they are dominated by the myth of Work. His profound piece of categorization, *Propaganda*, can be used by the propagandist as a textbook. In a corporate bourgeois society it serves almost no negating function.

Propaganda and Social Control

The individual, as spearhead or organizer or prime mover, may appear to be the basic unit in the creation of an institution of the bourgeois technology—a corporation, a school, a welfare department. He is not; no individual in his role as institution creator functions alone. All the values a man or woman might bring to the creation of an institution within a hegemonic system have been formulated, one might say programmed, within the individual by the hegemony, that is, by its propagandists. The very need to institutionalize is a product of linearity, of retentive individualism. (Attempts can be and have been made to avoid institutionalization. Disposable art in the mid-1960's, for example, might have been a transcension of institutionalized art, except that it itself was easily institutionalizable, and therefore quickly institutionalized. The inexpensive Styrofoam molds of Les Levine are exemplary.) The basic structures of a series of social values will be built up of the secondary mythomorphic forms. These forms came into existence out of the evolving needs of a society. Myths, through their agents (their spearheads, conceptualizers, organizers, and so on), help create institutions.

Most new institutions, like the more abstract myths that lie behind them, are originally creations of the concrete realities which lie behind the primary myth of History. As a new institution evolves to a point where it can validate its existence, its structure becomes frozen in time and the myth of Science becomes its new protector. In its early days its proponents had to act as agitation propagandists, advertising its importance. In its mature days its adherents remain proselytizers only to a limited degree, and become to a greater extent the integration propagandists who demonstrate the valuable place of the institution in the society at large. In its early days the chances are good that the institution will be progressive, answering directly and organically the needs of its creators and their contemporaries. As it matures and becomes a social success the chances are good that its adherents, for whom it has now become a vested interest, will attempt to impose their institutions onto others whose needs may not be directly answered by the institution's intentions. In its postmature period, its decadent days, the institution becomes reactionary, not (usually) because it has changed in nature but rather because it has remained the same while material changes in society have eliminated or rendered far more complex those needs it was once intended to answer.

By its decadent days many a contemporary institution has served long, and often served well. From the perspective of the hegemony an institution which has worked in the past may reach a point where it is no longer viable in achieving a technological goal most cleanly and quickly. This in itself does not constitute grounds for its dismissal or destruction, however. A superannuated institution may well be retained for its image, its tradition, its sentiment—not because it is still helpful to the goals of the hegemony, but because its tradition is an excellent smokescreen behind which the economic power base of the society can continue to function freely.

A great disjuncture exists between the way in which the liberal/conservative hegemony functions and the image it provides for itself. A major task of the integration propagandist is to present an image of the state both to its low-level technicians and to those on its peripheries. This image will never be built up of false information; rather it will be comprised of the hopes, dreams, sentiments, fears, and especially, the traditions of the audience, mythomorphised. All of these will appear very real; some of them will be tangential to the real intentions of the hegemony, but none of them will be close to the activity center of a hegemony's economic institutions. The audience's hopes and fears and myths will in fact have been created by earlier versions of the state itself. The propagandist need not lie. His audience, a product of the myth of Science, will not ask the propagandist if the dreams and myths in question are still valid; seen from within the myth of Science, secondary myths and dreams do not change.

The disjuncture between the hegemonical technostructure's reality and its image leaves it free of external controls, controls which might be unconducive to its desired goals. The disjuncture between image and circumstances allows it to plan its own future in peace. The planning function of the technostructure is extremely important,[14] and a citizenry must remain unenlightened as to its activities. The existence of a planning function makes it clear that the technostructure is not only capable of self-change but knows that it must change in order to remain in control of changing social circumstances. To this extent the hegemonic power base engages in a version of the myth of History, in that it creates, often in radical fashion, institutions organic to its own ends. This participation in causing basic social change contradicts its propagandized image, that of a great immutable though constantly growing monolith most easily comprehensible from within the myth of Science. This latter is the image for the anesthetized citizen to believe in and for the disgruntled unanalytical citizen (the contextless "radical") to attack; it is the smokescreen for the outsider to cope with (to fence with impotently), while the technostructure itself continues happily elsewhere, planning according to its own new needs the institutions of the future. The ongoing institution chiefly responsible for the technostructure's peace of mind belongs to the integration propagandist.

There are two basic kinds of institutions which serve

the goals of the hegemony. The first is the sort discussed above, created by and for the hegemonic state. The second existed prior to the liberal/conservative society and must be reformed by it if the society intends to use it. No all-pervasive society like bourgeois corporate capitalism can afford to allow a major institution to exist within its bounds the basic values of which stand apart from or, worse, are in opposition to the society's own. Over the period of time during which the newly pervasive society comes to power it must infiltrate each pre-existent institution and either destroy or transform it to its own ends. A potentially pervasive society can prosper only if it succeeds in taking over or destroying pre-existent institutions.

Toward these ends it needs allies, and it will find them best by creating self-justifying public opinion. Even so large a phenomenon as a mythomorphic form can be manipulated through public opinion. The dominant image from the Hero myth, the hero figure itself, was adapted to conform with the Nation myth: the soldier of fortune became a military hero fighting for race and homeland. The military hero finally died off, often literally, in World War I to the extent that in World War II—a conflict propagandized into appearing ideologically anti-imperialistic for the Allied Powers (Hitler's war was expansionist-nationalistic)—he could not even be propagandized back into existence. He died in 1918, battling appropriately enough a too-powerful military technology. Heroes of all nations lost out and died; technology was the only victor. The mid-twentieth century hero fought with liberal/conservative technology as his ally, or he failed. He was subservient to the hegemony, structurally its servant, and his forms of action were built from components of the myth of Work. The James Bond form of hero, who serves the hegemony and utilizes its technological products in his heroics, is the most successful hero. He is much less personally, individualistically heroic than the eighteenth century soldier of fortune, a man on his own. But the James Bond form of hero was

satisfactory to its audience; he was demanded by the
audience as fulfillment of the need for a hero within the
hegemony. The audience queued up and paid well for
the chance to be propagandized.

The propagandist, realizing that public opinion is one
of his most powerful tools, uses it to break down potentially self-determinable and therefore dangerous historically evolved groups and institutions within the society,
or at least groups which had been organic because they
once answered specific needs. Aristocracy is no longer a
visible institution; the various churches and the male-
dominated society are on their way out. The nuclear
family will largely disappear as a popular institution
because the hegemony's technology will render it unnecessary; the needs it once fulfilled will be satisfiable
elsewhere. Many of its potential and present participants
have already opted out, at least in the pervasive liberal/
conservative societies. All such institutions are first
broken down by agitation propaganda, the effect of
which is to force the participant to defend his acceptance
of, for example, the nuclear family as an institution. Few
can defend any phenomenon they have never analyzed,
always taken for granted; any well-constructed argument from the agitation propagandist which directs itself
to a historically evolved need (however partial) in his
audience will sound convincing. Then the integration
propagandist takes over; the deinstitutionalized citizen
in the audience and in the society, newly deprived of his
or her old categories, now at a loss, is easily introduced
to a world of new protoinstitutions. She or he will accept
such a thing because there is nothing else. The proto-
institution may be no more or less organic than were the
institutions of the old world. But because the protoinsti-
tution is reinforced by the integration propagandist it
will *seem* to be more, or even completely, historically
based and valid.

A person participates organically in the new institution to the extent that it is necessary, according to the
hegemony, for him or her to do so. The propagandist

creates an awareness of the positive value of collections
of bourgeois individuals. These are not collectives in any
communal sense. Rather, they are comprised of individuals fragmented off from each other, from their work,
and from the daily institutions they had known. These
collections will be arbitrarily associated groups, comprised of individuals brought together with no loyalty to
each other, manipulable directly by the hegemony. The
apparent form of a pseudoinstitution may be similar to
that of an evolved institution: the suburb or bedroom
community instead of the town; the trailer park retire-
ment village instead of the extended family; swinging
singles, or withdrawn communes at the other extreme,
in place of the nuclear family; low-cost housing complexes instead of the historically developed ghetto.

But the pseudoinstitution will be recognizable intern-
ally by its individual components—these remain fragmented from each other. Fragmented components are
easily controlled by the propaganda of the hegemony
which brought them to their present state. The American
university provides a common example: the monopoly
capital state creates its university within the confines of
conservative/liberal economics and the openness of all
knowledge, the highest principles of the myth of Science;
the university hires its faculty within these confines; the
faculty uses and interprets texts in order to transform the
sometimes inquisitive adolescent into a student consistent
with these confines—one has to be, one is told, or one
won't get a job; and the student subsequently becomes a
member of the hegemonic base because he or she has
learned to fit these confines. The university has succeeded. At every step, it is controlled from outside by the
principles of the hegemony. The administrations usually, the faculties often, and many of the students before
they ever enter the university are part of the hegemony
and are subservient by its ideology. The principle of open
inquiry within the myth of History is rarely if ever
broached. Often, such inquiry has been condemned as
destructive to the social fiber (which it may be). There

is no university community, because its components are
themselves fragmented from each other, rather than col-
laborating or competing with each other. Loyalties are
economically determined and therefore controllable and
controlled from outside, according to the needs of the
hegemony. When, of seven university vice-presidents,
only one is the academic vice-president, the university
belongs to the hegemony *in toto.*

Especially in times of economic growth and so semi-
flexibility, such fragmented groups are easily controlled
by the implicit promise of increased income and so security within the state structure. The gay nineties, the roar-
ing twenties, the satisfied fifties (the opulent eighties,
when the minorities are "integrated"?) stand out as
moments of peace (the Korean War notwithstanding)
and prosperity, during which fragmented institutions
seemed whole to those looking at them from the outside.
A group looks whole for two reasons: virtually no activ-
ism from within the group makes it seem as if all is well,
and the properly propagandized image of a group makes
those outside it assume all is well. Placidity, like laughter, is catching. Making placidity catch on is the job of
the propagandist. He has the machinery for it, the mythomorphic forms to manipulate and the media of dissemination. He will not release that machinery.

But the propagandist is as much a property of the
myth of Science as he is its propagator. He therefore has
control over a large amount of propaganda-making machinery, and has only a very partial idea how to use it.
So he sets it into operation in accordance with time-
tested principles. He is no more willing to give up on
what has worked in the past—for reasons of pragmatism,
sentiment, and tradition—than are those in his usual
audience. When the specific piece of machinery he is
using produces printed material, he remains by and large
successful. Print has functioned in relatively unchanging fashion for some four hundred years, and still can
turn its audience's linearly programmed mind.

But visually transmitted information is different; its

machinery provides for the possibility of simultaneity. The simplest levels of simultaneity, mutual reinforcement and undercutting of information presented by sound and image, have already been mentioned. The most naïve form of simultaneity, sound/image, is also the most sophisticated that television has yet utilized. Simple simultaneity can largely be controlled. Complex simultaneity probably cannot, but very few examples have as yet appeared, so it is difficult to discern its controllability.[15] Most programming pretends, or assumes, that television is a linear medium and should be used for the rote translation of literary and journalistic materials into depictive form. Such programming does not take into consideration the nature or the psychology of perception. The propagandist implants linear structures within visual medium presentations because he does not know what else to do. He controls the machinery of the electronic media, and only thereby controls their content. But the contemporary propagandist does not possess a theory of content adequate to the electronic media.[16]

*The Fiction of Freedom and the
Pragmatic Truth of Leakage*

That the propagandist does not today possess a theory of media content is extraordinarily important. It is also important to realize that corporate capitalism's creation, possession, and distribution of an explicated theory of media content will not be forthcoming because it is impossible for the hegemony to publicize an analysis of the potential of especially the visual media and then retain control over the content implications of that analysis. The possibilities of media transmission of information are so great, the ability of, for example, television to present a plethora of information to a mass audience and to receive feedback information in exchange is so vast, that when it comes about no central power, no hegem-

ony, will be able to control information in a manner
necessary to transform that information into propaganda.
This raises a potential paradox: why will a fully
propagandized audience not continue to function according to the precepts of its learned lessons if it gains access
to increased information, let alone once it has full access
to available information? The resolution of the paradox
lies in the fragmenting nature of propaganda and its
ability to undercut doubt. When the citizen senses that
the information being served up to him or her is inadequate, she or he will question it only if he or she does not
stand alone in this inquiry, only if she or he is sure of not
looking foolish or naïve or out of place. If the propagandist can keep one from communicating this doubt to
fellow citizens, the doubt dies a quiet death. But if one is
in control of those media which can make a doubting
voice heard not only by the technostructure but also by
one's like-minded neighbors, then his or her uncertainty,
which had previously been only a minimal individual
side-product of propaganda, can become the material
basis for a unified reaction to, and critique of, those
powers which have theretofore held one in an oppressed
circumstance. Inquiry, too, is catching.

A hegemony's lack of control over information would
mean a lack of control over the audience to be formed by
that information if the hegemony is to achieve its privileged ends. The only methods for recapturing control
over an audience once broad-based dissemination of information has become possible are nondemocratic, and
liberal/conservative society, at least in its present forms,
does not appear prepared to discard the principles of
some form of parliamentary or representative democracy,
not even within the myth of Science. A consistent theory
of media content, broadcast at large to a mass audience,
constantly as if the theory were itself propaganda—
which to the extent that it serves a negating function, it
is, though of the agitative sort—would undermine first
the image and then the basis of the privileged hegem-

ony.[17] Hence such broadcasting cannot now be allowed, at least not with any kind of consistency. Occasional programming of such a theory, or content evolved from such a theory, may be permitted, because the liberal version of democracy comes dressed up as the marketplace of ideas (intermittently, if they are not too dangerous). Initially, such a theory would get lost in the sea of integration propaganda.

From the perspective of the hegemony's dominant classes, the greatest danger of a plethora of information presented through electronic media is that the audience need not be literate in order to receive it, or to send it. Literacy has been the key to the club, the first step into the privileges of liberal/conservative society. Illiteracy has been equivalent, in its effect and even in its meaning, to uncivilization. Illiterate, preliterate, subliterate, postliterate, literate: all these realities become meaningless in the face of communication through electronic media. But the horror on the part of the ruling classes is far greater than that the unwashed unread billions will enter the privileged world. For the availability, on all levels, of all known information, could well bring about the downfall of the dominance of the myth of Science, that mainstay of the economic control of monopoly capitalism over the vast majority of the world's people. The elimination of partisan (national, racial, any form of fragmenting) control over information is an inextricable and central prerequisite to relief from economic oppression. When the products of the technology are brought into the service of the working and out-of-work classes, the surplus value of these products returns to their producers and the technological state ceases to be an oppressive society. The worker must understand first the extent of his or her exploitation by the corporate privileged classes; only then will each begin to become aware that it is even possible to demand a part in controlling the products and services he or she is producing. Without an applied theory of media content, such an egalitarian society will not come about.[18]

The argument has been made that modern human beings are incapable of dealing with all the information available to them now. How by extension could one possibly cope if one was forced to deal with all information, if one had to deal with radicalized media communication? The response is twofold. First it must be said, with Ellul, that the very concept of "all information" is an impossibility. Indeed, the concept itself does not become a goal within the context of the myth of History. A theory which sees electronic media as egalitarian in structure and in potential function suggests an access to information and therefore to the technique needed to render such a medium open to each citizen. No dialectical theory would ask for all information; but every dialectical theory demands the *possibility of access* to all available information. It is the availability of certain information to a few and the denial of access to that same information to most others which gives power, most often economic power, to those who control and use that information. Secondly, access to all information eliminates the most exhausting element implicit in the contemporary barrage of information, its propagandistic partiality. In order to deal with propaganda, one must attempt to transcend it; often the tools or methods for such transcendence are not available. Too consistent failure can easily exhaust the single individual who attempts to cope. But having to cope with propaganda could become unnecessary; implicit in total access is the possibility of eliminating contradictions by having available the material necessary to resolve the relation between otherwise fragmenting pieces of information.

An applied egalitarian theory of media content is one of the basic institutions within the mythomorph of Synthesis. It is not yet possible, however, to function largely within this mythomorph. The contemporary question is not, How does one deal with a theory of media content, but rather, How can one avoid the distortions implicit in propaganda in order to work toward such a theory? Certain attempted answers are inadequate, though they do suggest directions. McLuhan, for example, dazzled the bourgeois mind in the sixties with his conceit, "the medium is the message"; his analysis is partial and correct, but for the wrong reasons. If the medium of television with its potential for simultaneity reduces itself to linear presentation, then he has taught us nothing except the importance of recognizing that each phenomenon has a form as well as a content, which we knew though may have momentarily forgotten in our dealings with this still relatively new electronic medium. The implication, beyond McLuhan, begins to come clear: television's proper content is not linearity, but dialectics.

And taking this hypothesis a step further, it becomes possible to understand why it has been so difficult to explain and to comprehend dialectical processes through the medium of linear print. The profound difficulties many have experienced in reading and understanding, for example, Hegel's *Phenomenology of Mind*—especially the introduction, which explains the nature of dialectical processes by using dialectical processes—are compounded because Hegel was limited to a linear medium of explanation. I do not mean to be at all facetious by suggesting that dialectics could perhaps be better explained to a linearly trained mind with an animated cartoon, a material depiction of abstract forces in opposition, coming into conflict, a dominant shape/force changing over a period of time so that in the end it could be negated by a newly evolved shape/force. Once the concept of dialectical relationship has become legitimized as an alternative to consequentiality, its adaptation to daily situations and concrete history becomes a great deal easier for many linearly trained positivistic citizens. Dialectical materialism ceases to mystify when one attains tools for its comprehension. The limitation of "the medium is the message" is that it was intended for an audience that believes in the myth of Science; the glib dictum all too easily distracts the mind from the additional analysis of which one is capable.

Ellul's attempts, too, are inadequate, and sometimes

counterproductive. His refusal to engage in a critique of
the society and the propagandistic processes he describes
is disturbing. His hope in "a high intelligence, a broad
culture, a constant exercise of the critical faculties, and
full and objective information" as the "best weapons
against propaganda" (p. 111), his plea for understanding
what one reads, are simply inadequate, as he himself
finally concedes, in the face of total propaganda. Individual reaction of any sort is insufficient. One can still have
sympathy for the possibilities of the individual intellect
in terms of the dialectical content the intellect can provide. But unless that dialectical content can appropriate
a mass medium, it will be sweetly choked to death by
the all-pervasive hegemonical propaganda outlets.[19]

The success of the liberal/conservative state is based on
its ongoing ability to portray a minimally blemished
image of the apparently free society. Its most vociferous
critics, sometimes even its best, are provided with economic rewards, given stable positions in universities, and
write intelligent books which become best sellers. They
pass upward into success, into places of power. But this is
power as defined by the oppressive hegemony itself,
power in a technostructure where, as Galbraith has
shown, no one has real power because everyone joins in
the making of predetermined policy.

Nonetheless, an image sometimes has a tendency to
change the nature of the institution for which it was
intended as a smokescreen. Depicting and condemning
student or labor radicalism in a self-proclaimed free
society implies the portrayal and pretense at least of an
analysis of such action, some of which can prove attractive to some members of the audience. So the image can
create results in the audience not intended by the propagandist. These side effects are called *propaganda leakage*. Within the myth of Science, side effects are ignored;
within the myth of History, they are the dialectical
chickens which later come home to hatch negations. In
a socialist democracy (not a *social* democracy), the state
educates the population by providing it with the tools

and methods which, when applied to the state, will reshape it to fit the needs of its citizens. Both the desired
effects and the side effects of the state's programs serve
to determine the direction the socialist democracy takes.
A technological system would be one of the tools of socialist democracy; it will function, when it exists, within
the myth of History.

But the hegemonically privileged pseudodemocracy
exists within the myth of Science. It attempts to function as a closed system: The state controls the machinery
of propaganda which is used to create the public opinion
by which its citizens function and are moved to the kind
of action which a citizen's sense of democracy tells him
leads to the people's control over their governing state
(which controls the machinery of propaganda which
. . .). But this apparently closed circle takes place in
time, and time is the context within which people live
and create processes of change that introduce side effects,
or leakage. To discover points of leakage it is only necessary to experience the circle analytically and then examine any point of public juncture. Here we have been
concerned primarily with the propaganda juncture, with
the kinds of information the hegemony provides its public; but the arbitrarily closed system can be examined at
any of its points of stress. Leakage provides the handle
on which to hang the beginnings of an analysis. It also
provides the material for establishing alternative propo-
sitions. And the analysis of contradictions at any one
point of stress results in a different comprehension of and
a recognition of weaknesses in all points of stress.

The single largest area of leakage in the propaganda
machinery is the gap between the potential for information dissemination by the audio/visual media, and their
practice. It is no accident that many an easy technological advance has not yet been made. The manufacture of
cheap videotape equipment for a popular market, like
the invention of devices for keeping old oil freighters
from breaking apart on the shoals or the development of
safety devices for automobiles, has not yet come about

because it does not satisfy the economic needs of monopoly capitalism. Insurance payments received on disheveled tankers are more desirable than the expense of saving a cargo; the freedom of barreling down the highway is more satisfying when it dares death; and most intellectuals wishing to say something antagonistic to the ruling classes have been taught they can say it more properly, and less obtrusively, in print. Technical control of electronic media, as we are still propagandized into believing, is anti-intellectual. But electronic communication technology itself has served as the basis for a leak-through which some who are not wholly propagandized have discovered and may begin to apply. Leakage is inevitable in any system based on a belief that the myth of Science can function in absolute terms.

This takes us back then to the beginning, and to the question of the goals of information. Rivet, McLuhan, and Ellul agree that information leads to freedom. Though it was necessary to begin with the concept of freedom as a dialectical hypothesis, it now becomes equally necessary to suggest that freedom for individuals itself is a fiction, a created concept useful for our purposes primarily to evaluate and then go beyond three conceptions of the relation between literacy and information. It is important, before taking this discussion primarily to theatrical phenomena, to state explicitly that freedom and causality are abstract concepts and segments of the same continuum. Even a metaconception of reality is economically, socially, and psychologically determined. On the level of meta-analysis, the question of this sort of freedom becomes negligible, and the possibility of dialectical perspective takes its place. Freedom from propaganda is also a minimal goal, since dialectical perspective permits control over propaganda. With such perspective it is also possible, as the basis of proselytizing mass transcendence of hegemonic control, to reject Rivet's linear form and fragmented content; to borrow McLuhan's misapplied conception of wholistic form and to reject his fragmented (his lack of) content; to reject

Ellul's linear form and to apply his principle of total content; and to do all of this in order to conclude with a dialectical form applied to critical content and to achieve dialectical control over media which are egalitarian in structure and in their potential value.

Chapter Three

THREE THEATERS OF PROPAGANDA

It was about 1936 that Bertolt Brecht wrote the following:

> ... bad as it may sound, I have to admit that I cannot get along as an artist without the use of one or two sciences. This may well arouse serious doubts as to my artistic capacities. People are used to seeing poets as unique and slightly unnatural beings who reveal with a truly godlike assurance things that other people can only recognize after much sweat and toil. It is naturally distasteful to have to admit that one does not belong to this select band ... but I must say that I do need the sciences. I have to admit, however, that I look askance at all sorts of people who I know do not operate on the level of scientific understanding: that is to say, who sing as the birds sing or as people imagine the birds to sing. I don't mean by that that I would reject a charming poem about the taste of fried fish or the delights of a boating party just because the writer had not studied gastronomy or navigation. But in my view the great and complicated things that go on in the world cannot be adequately recognized by people who do not use every possible aid to understanding.[1]

With this gentle admonition in mind, one can attempt to examine the ways in which theater both is and uses propaganda.

As there are two basic kinds of propaganda, plus a basic method, essentially propagandistic in function, of overcoming propaganda, there are also three theaters (in the sense of performance) of propaganda. This examination and critique will first separate these types one from the other. To a great extent the success of each dominant type of theater is dependent on its ability to make use of characteristics taken from one or both of the other types. But the examination of such typological contamination must wait until later. The three types of theater may be categorized as:

1. The theater of agitation propaganda
2. The theater of integration propaganda
3. The theater of dialectical propaganda.

For the sake of clarity, the discussion which follows shall make only a historical distinction among the several media through which these types of propagandistic theater are presented. That is, if we take as our center of interest the relation between the several theaters of propaganda and their audiences, the effect of the one on the other, then the only differences between stage theater, film theater, and television theater are technological. The developments of live, cinematic, and electronic theater each have their place in the history of dramatic presentation, and so too their audiences have differed historically. But for present purposes this critique is interested only in their simultaneous availability at the beginning of the last quarter of the twentieth century as theaters of propaganda. To be sure, these several technologies still today reach their audiences under differing immediate circumstances, and later it will be important to clarify the psychic processes by which members of an audience are affected by different media. But here a consideration of the ideological content of these theaters of propaganda is important.

First it must be clear that all theater is propagandistic. As it presents partial information (the play's aesthetic perspective) and takes an ideological position in relation to that information, no play can avoid its propagandistic role. The nature of that propaganda can be determined, and the play thereby better understood, only when each member of the audience has recognized this essential fact and begins to question whom, as propaganda, the play serves. Thereafter one can begin to speak of valuable or of productive propaganda.

Sometimes propaganda is made within the play for the purposes *of* the play. At other times the play propagandizes an ideology without an awareness on the part of the playwright or of the production that the presentation is implicitly laden with values which the play is propagandizing. In either case there are processes at work within the play with intentions to support, to attack, or to change an audience's perception of material reality. The playwright as a disseminator of information in dramatic form plays a propagandistic role. The nature of the propaganda determines the ideology of the role.

The most obvious, because the most visible, kind of propagandistic theater is the theater of agitation propaganda. Agitation propaganda can be part of theatrical performance or of a more general consciousness-manipulation process—all of agitation propaganda contains a strong theatrical element. It is usually a propaganda of negation, standing in opposition to popularly recognized institutions. Ellul speaks of agitation propaganda this way: "It is most often subversive propaganda and has the stamp of opposition. It is led by a party seeking to destroy the government or the established order" (p. 71). Ellul goes on to point out that agitation propaganda can also be used by state-controlled media to galvanize the people of that state against another state, as would be the case in the preparation for war.

The most visible theater of agitation propaganda was the radical theater movement of the sixties. Such theater had as its intention the desire to point to and depict social problems previously invisible or at least unexamined by the citizenry. Agitation propaganda, presented theatrically, participated in raising its audiences' consciousnesses to a point where social and political problems took on shape and immediacy. So there was a theater of agitation propaganda against U.S. participation in the war in Vietnam, against such forms of domestic blindness as racism and later sexism—against exploitive institutions in general. It was a theater which at its best excited its audiences if not to action at least to an awareness they had previously lacked. It and any theater of agitation propaganda have the power to render in concrete form circumstances which to that moment had remained parts of a quietly undifferentiated, generalized daily reality.

The most frequent and yet the most often invisible propagandistic theater is the second, the theater of integration propaganda. Since integration propaganda is a devious phenomenon, difficult to discern and often problematic to define, it can perhaps be best discussed in terms of its purpose and within its medium of presentation. That is, if it is to suggest that all is as well with the world as it is ever going to get; that the best way for an audience or a society to cope is within carefully delineated boundaries, clear-cut channels and categories; that one should accept the ideological precepts of the society within which one functions even to the point of never understanding there is a created ideology within the precepts, then the vessel that contains this metainformation must have discernible structures. It is valuable to recall Ellul's words: integration propaganda, he says, "is a self-producing propaganda that seeks to obtain stable behaviour, to adapt the individual to his everyday life, to reshape his thoughts and behaviour in terms of the permanent social setting." Integration propaganda is long-term in nature, and most importantly, it is produced in far greater quantity by the social hegemony, those who passively accept the ideology of a society and function actively within it—teachers, preachers, newsmen, filmmakers, social workers, playwrights, psychologists: any who are in the business of affecting the general consciousness—than it is by those relatively few bureaucrats who are actively paid by their governments to make, in the traditional sense, a society's propaganda.

Just as integration propaganda is all-pervasive, so too is its theater. Most of the theater we see is the theater of integration propaganda: most of television, most of film, most of the successful work written for the stage is a form of integration propaganda. Its purpose is to support the dominant ideology as that ideology has formulated itself in the minds of as many in its audience as possible. As response to the satisfaction nurtured in each member of, for example, the television audience by seeing his or her own personal individual private beliefs reinforced— "Yes, Kojak or Lucas Tanner or John-Boy handled that just as I would hope I'd be able to"—each such audience member is supposed, finally, to find sympathy as well for Di-Gel or Ultrabrite or a Matador. The extent to which specific members of the audience then and there decide to buy the product does not prove the success or lack of success of the particular piece of integration propaganda; what counts in the end is whether the audience has been sufficiently reinforced to come back, to watch more episodes, to associate the pleasure of the integration propaganda's story and ideology with the product offered for sale, and finally to accept both propaganda and product without demur. I cite this apparent tangent, the relation between TV ratings and product sales, because ratings and sales are two of the better ways of measuring the success of a piece or pieces of television theater as integration propaganda, that is, as pieces of dramatic narrative which seek to obtain stable behavior and which try to adapt the individual to his daily life, tense and contradictory though it may be.

The most difficult theater to create, though not at all difficult to understand, is the theater of dialectical propaganda. It is a theater which attempts to demystify, by depicting separately, interactively, and always clearly, the basic elements which comprise a confused social or historical situation. This is the science of dialetical materialism, of Ellul's myth of History, brought to dramatic presentation. Brecht started by calling his version of such a theater "epic," a category I would avoid—first, because he quite rightly finally labeled it dialectical; and secondly, because I want, further on, to suggest other aspects of a theater of dialectical propaganda, such as a theater of future alternatives, a programmatic or utopic theater. Here, in speaking of dialectical propaganda, Ellul's use of the term *propaganda* has to be modified somewhat. Ellul has explained that both integration and agitation propaganda are methods of presenting, not falsehoods, but partial truths, so that the perpetrators of such propaganda can gain control over their audiences in order to manipulate them. Dialectical propaganda and its theater, on the other hand, utilize information in the manner John Berger describes in his discussion of impressionist painting. A painting, he explains, is a partial presentation of reality. (In this respect it can of course serve as agitation or integration propaganda.) But, Berger goes on, "I emphasize like this the relativity of what any one of us sees at a given moment, not in order to allow everyone to claim their own 'reality,' not to suggest that reality itself is unknowable, but rather to emphasize that reality is far more complex than any single view of appearances. No work of art can do justice to the whole complexity of reality. Every work of art is a simplification based on a convention. The convention itself emphasizes a particular aspect of nature in accordance of the interests of the particular social group or class that has created it."[2]

In this respect a theater of dialectical propaganda, as a theater of cognitive clarification, will present detailed and structured information through a dramatic medium in order to depict, for its audience, circumstances not previously understood. It will demystify relationships between individuals and institutions, individuals and individuals, institutions and institutions, so as to show, first, the nature of passions and of economic and social laws, and second, to demonstrate methods by which human beings can control both themselves and their institutions. In their introduction to *Monopoly Capital*, Baran and Sweezy emphasized the essence of dialectical propaganda: "One type of criticism we would like to answer in advance. We shall probably be accused of exaggerating. It is a charge to which we readily plead guilty. In a very real sense the function of both science and art is to exaggerate, provided that what is exaggerated is truth and not falsehood."[3] A theater of dialectical propaganda exaggerates its clarifications of previously mysterious circumstances and relationships in order to play these off against established misrepresentations, unexamined conventions, and, increasingly often, outright falsehoods.

The theater of agitation propaganda, in its pure form, is an attempt to make a single comment about a circumstance or relationship. Such a theater is capable therefore of an extremely powerful short-term shock effect, striking at the heart of an issue with piercing accuracy. Sometimes guerilla in nature, sometimes enclosed in traditional trappings, the theater of agitation propaganda is at its best when it is brief in duration. The destruction of a plastic motel room in Jean-Claude van Itallie's *Motel* was an agitation-propaganda depiction of unrelieved and, within the play, unperturbing violence. Michael McClure's *The Beard* pitted Billy the Kid against Jean Harlowe in a sexual devastation of heroic images. These were in-theater productions, designed for audiences willing to pay to be scandalized. In *The Beard*, the secondary myth of the Hero (and Heroine) was relieved of its mystified trappings by denying to its protagonists the structures which give dramatic power to the hero figure: external perspective, escape from or integration into society. Billy and Jean are reduced to an erotic Gogo and Didi.

But agitation-propaganda performance often took place, still sometimes takes place, in noninstitutionalized theatrical performance conditions, and is perhaps at its most effective under such circumstances. A guerilla theater group carrying large plastic bags, each filled with a "dead American soldier" whose simulated guts were dripping out through holes in the plastic—a procession of these through a suburban shopping center, to-

gether with sprightly military music, comprised a southern California production called *Body Count*. This was
pure agitation propaganda, in design juxtaposing two
deeply contradictory circumstances. Its purpose was to
shock and thereby to expose, and in this it succeeded.
But many less successful examples of agitation propaganda succeed only in antagonizing their audiences
without demystifying for these audiences the contradictions the plays and skits depict. Here precisely is the
danger of a theater of agitation propaganda: that its perpetrators have, simultaneously, little understanding of
the content material of their plays and little understanding of the spectrum of their audiences' tastes and
tolerance thresholds. While a sense of outrage, carefully
controlled, can be turned into excellent theater, many
agitation-propaganda theaters took, and take, neither
themselves nor their plays, and consequently not their
audiences either, through the processes which would
make a parking-lot suburbanite understand his or her
relationship to culpability in military and economic warfare. Not that an agitation-propaganda play should be a
lecture; *Body Count* succeeded by uniting two sides of
war, murder and patriotism, in a single scene of pleas-
antly recognizable music and tangible plastic bags enclosing the corpses of once-living Americans. Many in
the audience made the associations themselves; they
were outraged, and through their outrage they understood. When, however, a play causes outrage alone, then
an audience can easily deny the ideological accusations
within its content, and all too often because that content
was badly presented. It will have been badly presented
because it was poorly understood by those participating
in the production.
    In order to demystify the processes of the theater of
integration propaganda, it would be valuable to examine
a specific example, one of the finest pieces of cinematic
integration propaganda recently created, the film version
of the original of *The Godfather*. This is a highly seduc-
tive vehicle for audience manipulation, and its financial

and critical success speaks to its success as integration propaganda. The film, like the novel which preceded it, sets up the Mob, the Mafia, as an alternative system of social justice within the larger American society, a system extremely competent in coping with those contradictions which the external world either ignores or cannot handle. The undertaker at the beginning of the film asks for death for the two men who beat and raped his daughter and ruined her attractiveness; the Godfather refuses to kill but has them beaten in vengeance. Enzo the baker asks a political favor which will keep from deportation the immigrant young man his daughter loves; the Godfather can arrange it politically. Johnny the singer wants a movie career, and the Godfather provides. In each case the Godfather, Don Corleone, would at this early point in the film be an updated Robin Hood figure, were his subjects and their requests somewhat less selfish. Nonetheless Corleone's actions, together with the colorful simultaneous ethnicity of the intercut marriage of his daughter, establish him as a sympathetic though perhaps ruthless alternative force. The audience need not reconceive the Mafia as totally Robin Hood in nature, just as it need not see Don Corleone as a hero because he refuses to deal in dope (Don Corleone, ever pragmatic, does not wish to lose the favor of his political friends).

It is appropriate that virtually all the popular critics in the bourgeois journals found Marlon Brando's Don Corleone an attractive person. Arthur Knight in *Saturday Review*: "Two sides of the Don are thus exposed immediately—warm ties with his own family and his relationship with the 'family' that pays him obeisance in return for anticipated favours." Or Richard Schickel in *Life*: ". . . that dumb-shrewd, tough tender dialogue!! If real hoods don't talk this way, they ought to . . . everyone concerned with this film understands . . . that the movie gangster has traditionally been a tragic hero." Or *America*, sponsored by the Jesuits of the United States and Canada, in speaking of the ending of the film as " . . . a tender loving family portrait of Don Corleone and his infant grandson playing together in the garden of his estate." Arthur Knight said, similarly, "In *The God-father* we are dealing with people—home-loving, tightly knit, folksy people—who also happen to kill a lot."

Outlawry, especially early in the movie, is made to look attractive. The first two acts of violence in the film are inflicted on, rather than committed by, the Corleones, reinforcing their image as victims. When at last they act it is, for the audience, something of the revenge of the downtrodden—though not overly so, for it is important that at the end the Corleones be integrated into mainstream America as powerful equals, and that this integration be, in the mind of the audience, desirable.

The evolution of values in the film takes the audience from the semiapparent Robin Hood alternative to the fusion of outlawry and blatant capitalism. This fusion seems to dissolve all the contradictions that provide the film's tensions—everyone will supposedly live happily ever after. Only in retrospect does the alternative system of justice and action represented by the Family become discomfiting; mob violence, as even the popular critics noted, is seen as the extension, or the dark side, of American capitalism. Michael, the next head of the Family, defends his father, saying he is "powerful just like any powerful man." Kay, the girl Michael will marry, responds, "Do you know how naïve you sound? Senators and presidents don't have people killed." The irony would hang heavy except for some expert photography and cutting. But at this point the alternative façade is no longer needed—the Corleone money will be used to buy into Las Vegas: gambling, vice, popular holiday pleasures. Las Vegas was, after all, the home of the last of the self-made men.

The relationships among integration propaganda, filmic presentation, and audience reaction are perhaps best illustrated by the final scene but one, the intercutting between the baptism of Michael Corleone's first godson and the brutal murders of the opposition families. Audience reaction to the scene is dependent on the larger reaction—to a hundred and seventy minutes of viewed material culminating with the baptism/murders intercut. This latter reaction, like reaction to any form of craft for the purpose of integration propaganda, in turn depends on the larger political attitudes of the audience: is this penultimate scene in bad taste, is it social criticism, or is it merely icing on a cake?

The conservative elements in the audience—staunch Catholics, say, or members of the Italian-American Anti-Defamation League (many Italian-Americans boycotted the film)—might well and justifiably find the scene nasty, unfair, and insulting. From their perspective such a condemnation would be a proper appraisal.

A conservative/liberal audience could easily find, and usually has found, the penultimate scene aesthetically pleasing, a slap at the hypocritical sides of the most unbending of orthodox Christianities by associating it directly with the villainous, but by the audience largely unexamined, capitalism with which the Mob has, by this time in the film, been fused.

Very few, if any, in the conservative/liberal audience will see this scene as the acme of the film's implicit integration propaganda purposes. Out of lack of perspective, the first group will ignore it. The second will accept it as an entertaining film which, as most of the reviewers —themselves thereby participants in the processes of integration propaganda—have said, humanizes the mobsters. But the ideological identification of so-called humanized mobsters with flexible and so, in the film, humanized capitalism, and both with a sense, which pervades the audience, of seeing in Michael Corleone a model for toughness—these taken together testify to the success of the film as a vehicle for an integration propaganda which depicts bourgeois capitalism's supposed vitality.

Family peace and intermob murder serve as visible symptoms of the material contradictions which provide the film's tensions. The early part of the film juxtaposes these contradictions in apparently irreconcilable fashion

—economic control means elimination of competing families, and these families have a tendency to fight back. The concluding attempt at reconciliation, going away to peaceful Vegas, is an artificial conjunction which essentially avoids the issue; for the purpose of the film this imposed conjunction is liberal titillation of the happily-ever-after sort, going off appropriately enough to the wide-open if no longer wild West—a cosmetic cover-up that tries to hide an unfulfilled human need for peace behind the momentary relief of escape. On an immediate level, the ending is liberally satisfactory. Even when Michael has to lie to his wife, denying that he had his brother-in-law killed, the image of the gangster as lonely tragic hero remains to reflect the readily acceptable, unexamined Dilemma of Modern Man, or some equivalent existential nonsense imposed on the audience by an earlier network of integration propaganda.

The film was a great success for a number of reasons. First, it suggests the potential popularity of a less alienated system of justice and order. But this suggestion takes place, for the largest part of the audience, only on the subliminal level. Few could be willing consciously to admit to so basic a displeasure as alienation contaminating their lives unless they are carefully led into a different, far more critical awareness. This does not happen: at all major points *The Godfather* opts to reintegrate the viewer and the perceived action back into the audience's contextual system.

Second, the film is a success because it has been called a success by reviewers. This validification first undercuts and subsequently reinforces the twin alienations usually imposed on personal judgment by the integration propaganda institutions of a bourgeois society: on the one hand the remark, "I liked it (or didn't like it), *but that's just my opinion*"—a venal limitation secreted elsewhere and at another time within the mind of each member of the audience so as to anesthetize his subsequent critical powers and to amputate any possible arm of action resulting from even a feeble critique; and on the other hand the general mistrust and dismissal of critics who, everyone in the audience suspects, are controlled by the media complex which uses them to popularize its products. But, when members of the audience find themselves in agreement with critical praise, their relief that reviewers have verbalized the general audience sentiment builds on the pleasure given by the patterns within the movie to create in many in the audience so strong an advocacy of the film and all it represents that subsequently they themselves become tiny instruments of integration propaganda. And part of the *pleasure* of integration propaganda is to find oneself in agreement with most other members of the audience. To be a member of a collection is confused with being a member of a collective.

Third, the film is a success because it exemplifies a high awareness of the demands of professional filmmaking. The work of Puzo and Coppola is completely consistent with the manufactured myth of existential impotence (the Dilemma of Modern Man being the context from within which the novel was written and the film made). To be sure, under certain circumstances existential impotence could provide an almost perfectly adequate analysis of the film. But there is one major inadequacy to such a myth: the myth of existential impotence avoids dealing with that element of analysis which other earlier bits and pieces of integration propaganda have convinced members of the audience they don't much need anyway, *the sense of historical evolution in the value systems of societies and so in the lives of their citizens.* If late bourgeois capitalism is the basis of the audience's ideology and if that ideology seems to be absolute, if the only kind of change possible takes place within Ellul's myth of Science and means merely more and better of the same, then the historical amelioration of social circumstances never becomes an issue for the audience. Then Michael Corleone's conversion to his father's way of life can be understood as the need for each man to commit himself, in an existential universe, to any world he finds highly sympathetic (for reasons of simplicity, or responsibility, or love, or hate, or ped- agogy, or fun, or whatever). That world is best in which one receives the most comfortable mediated positive re- sponse to one's actions: for one is always caught up, synchronically, in the system one has learned life in.

Without historical perspective, the synchronic defini- tion of social values becomes an existential absolute. Historical perception is the form of consciousness which it is the duty of integration propaganda, and its theater, to destroy. At this film's moment in time, law and order fights against organized crime and is depicted unappeal- ingly. But the viewer knows the film exaggerates, and anyway things are better now. The viewer has it both ways: immediate dangerless titillation, and the relief of distance. And at the same time, contemporary law and order remains democratic and generous enough to allow the showing of this film, which depicts police as corrupt and certain mafiosi as attractive generous people. Even if there are some problems, these will be solved soon. So the audience lives in a good world after all. The happily- ever-after final solution is nearly at hand. The more tra- ditional villains as depicted by the film—Sonny, who loses his temper, the last generation of fingermen, even the old capo Don Corleone—they are all dead. Now, as members of a bourgeois capitalist society, necessarily the same society as that of most in the audience, the Cor- leones will become respected citizens in Las Vegas, their children will go to the best schools and one day will marry non-Italians, and enter and control politics, there- by completing their participation in a larger North American society. Michael Corleone has already married Kay Adams.

The theater of dialectical propaganda, on the other hand, allows no such historical mystification of categor- ies. At its best, as in two examples from its most powerful practitioner, Bertolt Brecht, it both demonstrates the methods by which a bourgeois theater of integration propaganda beclouds the differences between truth and crime, honesty and business, awareness and self-delusion, and examines the causes for the possibility of such easy confusion. The purest example of a theater of dialectical propaganda is the Lehrstück *The Measures Taken*. Unencumbered by characterization or the trappings of a plot, it depicts the concrete moments of a dialectical advance, the testing of a young comrade through actual revolutionary work and his ultimate failure. The play shows only a microscopic moment in the struggle for world revolution, and an unsuccessful one at that. But at the same time it focuses on the means by which each separate element in that moment contributes, infinitesimally yet irrevocably, to the largest part of the struggle, and the inevitable victory of its partisans. The action of the play is an acted-out narrative, presented by Four Agitators, of the young comrade's failure to forward the struggle because at each crucial moment the young comrade gives himself over only to the bourgeois virtues: pity, sympathy, self-respect, personal justice, individual action. The audience for the history depicted by the Four Agitators is the Control Chorus, who early on defines the criterion by which the case will be judged:

Who fights for communism must be able to fight and not to fight; to speak the truth and not to speak the truth; to perform services and not to perform services; to keep promises and not to keep promises; to go into danger and to keep out of danger; to be recognizable and not be recognizable. Who fights for communism has only one of all the virtues; that he fights for communism.

And tactics for any moment are defined by the analyzed concrete circumstances of that moment:

In time of extreme persecution and
The confusion of theory
The fighters depict the structure of the situation
And weigh the stakes and the possibilities.[4]

The Measures Taken, in explicit content, in implicit content and ideological structure, and in physical structure, leaves its propagandistic intentions in no doubt. At the same time, this unalloyed purity throws some doubt on the play's ability to function as effective popular propaganda. But the play was written as a Lehrstück, only for actors as its audience. There was for Brecht, when he wrote the play, no question of presenting it to a more general bourgeois audience. It lays bare the bones—laying bones bare is an excellent teaching device—of dialectical propaganda in dramatic form for those in the theater who, like the young comrade, have hearts which beat for the revolution but who have no programmatic control over their emotions, no restraint on their actions. Pure dialectical propaganda can, at this moment in bourgeois time, succeed only with a highly selected audience.

Transforming the intention to propagandize against bourgeois structures and for world revolution into a piece of theater intended for an audience without revolutionary commitment is the problem which makes a theater of dialectical propaganda the most difficult propaganda theater to create. If integration propaganda theater accepts and functions within the dominant ideology, then a dialectical propaganda theater in a bourgeois society will take as its goal one or both of two possibilities. It will present a step by step, institution by institution, process by process depiction and so clarification of a part or parts of the bourgeois world. Simultaneously it will present a critique of choices made by the protagonists within that world and will suggest alternative modes of action which might come about when a protagonist's class consciousness has reached the point at which he or she can sense the possibility of alternative action. Or, as in a programmatic theater of dialectical propaganda, a presentation of future alternative choices might leave the critique of a surrounding bourgeois society only implicit, and would instead stress the depiction of actions and institutions growing from a less alienated society. In a time of bourgeois hegemony, the problems for a theater of dialectical propaganda lie in comprehending, demystifying, and translating into dramatic language the essence of bourgeois institutions. A theater of programmatic propaganda would project human activity into, for example, an already postrevolutionary world wherein options for such activity remain open. There has not to this point been such a programmatic dialectical theater, though the presence of its fictional counterpart suggests there could be one.[5]

But Brecht provides us with a number of plays written specifically for a bourgeois audience, and of these *The Threepenny Opera* is especially pertinent because in its explicit content the narrative is essentially the same as that of *The Godfather*. That is, each of these two narratives describes the ideological proximity of crime and business, and each leads to a conclusion in which the greatest criminal is rewarded with the highest forms of respectability. Macheath's Las Vegas is the Castle Marmarel, plus an allowance of ten thousand pounds for its and his maintenance valid to the end of his days. Incidentally here but crucially in general, this thematic similarity between crime and big business underlines the dangers of limiting oneself to formal thematic analysis when dealing with the materials of propaganda. At the beginning of each of their tales, Macheath and the Godfather characters—in this case the old capo—participate in a successful life of crime; at the end of each, after a second marriage to a wife who accepts the husband's business as crime—by this time the Godfather figure is Michael Corleone—each story's protagonist is the heroic precursor of a new bourgeois propriety.

Such explicit similarity in content should emphasize the total difference in Brecht's and Puzo/Coppola's treatments. Where Puzo and Coppola are telling a tale undisturbed by analysis (analysis breaks the escapist pleasure continuity of a narrative for a bourgeois audience), Brecht depicts and juxtaposes moments central to the development of a criminal or a capitalist circumstance so that his audience can come to understand the similarities between Macheath and Peachum, two successful entrepreneurs operating, just barely, on opposite sides of the arbitrary line that separates crime from business. In addition, Brecht vibrates that line sufficiently to show, from the play's first moments, how easily a redefinition of both crime and business can take place: there are no charges against Macheath filed in Tiger Brown's Scotland Yard files; Polly handles Macheath's account books as she handles Peachum's.

The physical structure of the play as well—three acts, each made up of three scenes: the most literal dialectical form—attempts a clarification of the relationship of crime and business to bourgeois ideology. In act one, in Peachum's Beggars' Center, the play depicts the importance of image creation in the begging business, the necessity to divide begging territories so that beggars cover the whole of a market rather than competing with each other, the need for the beggar to pay interest on Peachum's original outlay of begging equipment—in short, analyzed parts of the workings of a smoothly run monopoly. Juxtaposed in scene two are the parallel workings of specifically criminal syndicalism: once more a division of the city into territories, the authorities who have been bought off, here all within the context of the culmination of romantic love—that is, the action takes place at Macheath and Polly's marriage feast. In scene three the confrontation of Mrs. Peachum, as the representative of capitalism's moral side, with Polly, as one who has gone over to crime while under the sway of romantic love, results in a finale which explains the uncertainty of human circumstances in a world where struggle is all-pervading, despite the attempt to conceal misery behind the cosmetic façade of romantic love.

Similarly, act two presents a tripartite structure in which Polly's love for Macheath is reduced to her business partnership with him, Macheath's love for Polly is reduced to his desire for the sexual possession of any woman, and these two abstractions find their common

ground in the only true love of the play, Peachum's for
his daughter Polly—since Peachum needs Polly's intelligence in his business, his love has only an uncomplicated
economic base, and so can remain pure. Act three sets up
the failure of social institutions—capitalism in the person of Peachum first undermining justice in the person
of Brown and then recreating justice in capitalism's own
image—and pits social failure against the failure of individual institutions—the marriages of Lucy and Polly
to Macheath, and their meaninglessness. This mutual
negation takes the play to its third act finale, in which
the audience is shown that the bourgeois ideals have now
failed utterly; justice, individuality, romantic love, security are all impossible. This failure is also the simultaneous conclusion, Brecht expected his audiences to
understand, of the structural relationship between the
first and second acts: when the uncertainty of individual
possibilities in a bourgeois world is confronted by the
certainty of economic needs—here Peachum's—there is
no question but that the individual, even when like Macheath he is only semiattractive, must face certain destruction. Still, to open up once more the discussion of
alternative possibilities, Brecht superimposes salvation
onto the play. The ending, out of melodrama, the ruling
of a *regina ex machina*, transcends arbitrary legal control and individual impotence. Macheath goes free, and
the audience is left asking why.

Answering such a question is relatively simple when
the response can be taken out of the context of a theater
of integration propaganda, and when the purpose of the
play which preceded was to clarify the processes that
could lead also to the arbitrary rescue depicted by the
conclusion. That is, Macheath's execution and his last-
minute salvation are equal alternatives when the forces
partisan to each conclusion are equally negative, equally
socially destructive. When crime and capitalism do battle, no people's society can be the winner. If Macheath
dies, Peachum is victorious and the play sanctions capitalism's version of justice. If Macheath lives and is

knighted and pensioned, the play accepts crime's control
of justice. Shifting so effortlessly from the inevitability
of one finale to the arbitrariness of the other can deny
the validity of either.

This brings us to the contamination of one kind of
theater of propaganda by another. If *The Threepenny
Opera* were a bourgeois melodrama of the early twentieth century sort, in which the villain was only partly
evil and therefore capable of being saved, usually by
a heroine (here a Polly/Lucy combination apotheo-
sized in Elizabeth Regina), then Macheath's miraculous
eleventh-hour–fifty-ninth-minute pardon would be entirely appropriate: that which by the standards of bourgeois pity is good, even only partially good, must not be
allowed to perish. And for an audience trained to enjoy
integration propaganda theater, of which bourgeois
melodrama was one of the highest early twentieth century forms, Macheath's arbitrary rescue was not out of
place. For such an audience even a satire of integration
propaganda theater would not remove such a play from
the domain of integration propaganda theater. Satire
alone, as a process of negation, may well not be sufficient
to expand an audience's consciousness out of the sphere
of integration propaganda, out to an enlarged awareness
both of integration propaganda as a created construct
and of the powers which control it. In short, for an audience that sees Macheath as a tough/tender all-but-tragic
hero in a somewhat funny play, Brecht's intention of
using integration propaganda theater against itself has
failed.

But though there are dangers inherent when one kind
of theater of propaganda borrows from another for whatever purpose, there are also vast potential strengths.
Agitation-propaganda theater can, for example, begin
with an integration propaganda theater situation and
break it wide open with a single visual blow. The most
effective of integration propaganda theater often begins
by feigning an agitation-propaganda technique, the
tease, to present a problem or series of problems which

seem at first properly to deny certain values of the dominant ideology, and then reduces these problems to pulp by apparently solving them within the alternatives of the contextual society. Or it may borrow, in a very limited fashion, techniques from a theater of scientific clarification; it may indeed utilize such techniques to impose tension on an otherwise drab situation. The film version of *The Sand Pebbles* spent a great part of its time showing the workings of a riverboat engine, a momentarily elucidative presentation, but the process had no goal beyond titillation. The television adventure series "Mission Impossible" thrived on the precision and the clarity with which it worked out escape plots. Such family series as "The Waltons" and such of its more short-lived carbons as "Lucas Tanner" and "Sons and Daughters" shift viewers' emphasis of interest from a mechanical technological explication to a mechanical psychological display, they claim, of the workings of human beings both alone and in warm close contact with others. But when clarifying techniques are subsumed by a larger mystifying world, and when the production exists primarily to deny an examination of that larger world, then the piece of theater remains integration propaganda. Only a theater of dialectical propaganda, a theater of cognitive clarification, attempts to separate out from each other mystifying and contradictory elements in the minds of an often purposely confused bourgeois audience. With the help of one or two sciences a playwright can transform narrative theater intended to mystify into a narrative theater of explanation, a theater that uses every possible aid to understanding and so can be considered the theater of artists.

On the other hand, certain kinds of dramatic materials, such as those which supply the content of the next two chapters, not merely do not demystify the worlds of their audience, but to a considerable extent serve as integration propaganda for their hegemonic sponsors. For such kinds of drama, artistry can be evaluated in terms of the extent to which a given play, say *The Conspiracy* from

the Wakefield Cycle, or Beckett's *Endgame*, succeeds in
presenting, convincingly for its audience, the ideology of
its explicit or implicit sponsoring institutions.

Understanding the function of each play's propaganda
then becomes possible for a later audience. That is, it
becomes possible to see whether certain examples of
agitation propaganda are progressive or reactionary,
since there is, abstractly speaking, not necessarily an
ideology implicit in this kind of propaganda's agitational
nature. If a theater of agitation propaganda supports a
fascist cause, if it advocates, for example, the lynching of
liberals or of outsiders, or if it calls for a burning of texts
written by humane conservative authors, then the ideology of such a theater will differ entirely from that of a
revolutionary agitation propaganda, which would call
into question and perhaps depict ways of overcoming,
even through violent methods, antihuman situations,
totalitarian actions and injustices. For both such productions an agitation-propaganda intention would dominate
in the established relation between performance and
audience.

Somewhat similarly, it is possible for a theater of integration propaganda to serve either progressive or reactionary causes, though this as a possibility is far less
clear. It could be said that in a postrevolutionary society
integration propaganda's devices, including its theater,
are important to bring the society and the audience into
agreement with postrevolutionary values. But such an
image of a postrevolutionary society, while perhaps pragmatically an available alternative, is not attractive. A
fully radical humanist postrevolutionary society would
be best served, dramatically, by a theater of dialectical
propaganda. That is, its aesthetic and its social models
would best be those which depicted the *processes leading toward* what postrevolutionary ideology considered
valuable for the new society. Integration propaganda
and its theater are capable only of artificially imposing,
through repetition and consistency, any new (including
socialist postrevolutionary) values and institutions. By

definition, integration propaganda and its theater cannot take an audience or a society along a process by
which a society can learn to build its institutions through
conscious critique. The effort of integration propaganda
in post- and of course more in pre-revolutionary societies
is to break down the processes and possibilities for critique. Integration propaganda was, as we shall see, a
basic implicit and explicit program, on the part of the
Catholic Church, in its condoning and controlling the
ideology of late-medieval mystery plays. And such propaganda remains today a time-proven and pervasive phenomenon, most valuable for countering progressive
action and the constant battle against hegemonic inhu-
manity.

Chapter Four

CLASS STRUGGLE AND LATE-MEDIEVAL

INTEGRATION PROPAGANDA IN

THE WAKEFIELD MYSTERY CYCLE

Integration propaganda is much more than a twentieth century phenomenon. Historically it played its part whenever the agents of economic power sought, rhetorically or depictively, in the largest sense, to present their audiences with images of recognized positive value, images that were immediately or ultimately associated with allegiance to the state or the community. Vesting ultimate authority in natural law, in implicit patriotism, in common sense or personal experience can serve integration propaganda as easily as can the most obscure but mutually reinforcing institutions of, for example, a religious sort. Told for generations that their gods are merciless, or strong but benevolent, members of a society cannot conceive of their own deified anthropomorphizations in any other fashion. Therefore a relatively uncontaminated example or series of examples from dramatic history can prove valuable in exploring the service to which theater can be put by a powerful and subtle ruling class.

"I will not lose what I have made," says God at the beginning of *The Annunciation* (175),[1] the tenth play of the Wakefield Cycle of Mystery Pageants. Through his mouth speak the sponsors of the spectacle: more than the established church, more than the producing guilds (but including both these institutions), this is the voice

of the hegemony that produces good citizenry, of everyone intricately bound up with the prosperity of the community—Wakefield, like any *ville* or *Stadt* or town
where Europeans with something to lose express, here
verbally, their inner fears through a social (in this case
an artistic and theatrical) form. In the early centuries of
bourgeois life[2] an ever-increasing number of citizens
could identify with God's first words in the play (refer-
ring on the immediate level to Adam), ". . . I have made
all things of nought . . ." Times were changing, socially
something new and still very unclear was happening.
There was a sense of the new phenomenon being good,
and it was important not to lose out on its possibilities
even if most people could not explain it to themselves,
let alone define in precise historical terms what their
participation in this new phenomenon meant.

There was also a sense of danger: novelty challenges,
and in some cases is destructive to, the staid established
order. Part of the purpose of the mystery plays was to
cater to that sense of novelty; part of the purpose (not
necessarily conscious) of the plays' hegemonic sponsors
was to harness the novelty and turn it to the sponsors'
own ends.

A large historical perspective can provide a context for
this subsensory but emerging consciousness. It is helpful
to adapt, for an analysis of late-medieval drama, the development of basic value structures within historical
evolution, that is, within historical progress: individualism in the Roman Republic was the outgrowth of Greek
aristocratic/democratic individualism; this previous less
pure individualism was itself in dialectical balance between the future Roman individualist extreme and the
communality of the earlier city-states. In similar fashion,
the decline of Roman individualism evolved, both organically and violently, into Christian communality and
its equally communal economic counterpart, the feudal
hierarchy. Finally, carrying historical gloss to the point
where it affects the Wakefield play cycle, its sponsors,
and its audience, a new protoindividualism in the eco-

nomic and social life of the late fourteenth century began
to establish the concrete basis for specific aesthetic and
political novelties. This Anglo-European individualism
was already of an order higher than its paradigm in
democratic Greece (of which popular medieval consciousness was almost totally unaware): the democratic
fruit of Greek individualism had been reserved primarily
for the aristocratic minority, while late-medieval individualism was beginning to affect (or infect, depending
on one's ideological perspective) a far broader population. The institutions of early modern individualism
would soon open a Pandora's box of possibilities even,
economically, to some among the lowest classes. Conversely, the certain probability of political and economic
control through imposed hierarchies, a tradition a millenium old, would begin to pass away.[3] City life, self-
determination, exchange and wealth expressed predominantly in terms of capital rather than in terms of land,
and direct contact between man and God (only a century off as an institution, and already long present in
the heresies): these were some among the elements of the
new consciousness which was beginning to pervade the
daily lives of many a citizen at the beginning of the fifteenth century in bourgeois Europe.

Perhaps the analysis contained in an early essay by
Karl Marx, "On the Jewish Question,"[4] can clarify the
nature of this historical gloss, since the critique pertains
to the time of the Wakefield Cycle. Marx attempted to
describe the beginnings of postfeudal individualism as
both an essential negation to decadent feudalism and as
the beginnings of a new force, bourgeois in structure,
which was to be, ultimately, destructive to human nature
and to the political nature of human institutions. (Italics
are Marx's.)

> Political emancipation is at the same time the *dis-*
> *solution* of the old society, upon which the sovereign
> power, the alienated political life of the people, rests.
> Political revolution is a revolution of civil society.

What was the nature of the old society? It can be characterized in one word: *feudalism*. The old society had a *directly political* character; that is, the elements of civil life such as property, the family, and types of occupation had been raised, in the form of lordship, castle and guilds, to elements of political life. They determined, in this form, the relation of the individual to the *state as a whole*; that is, his *political* situation . . . the vital functions and conditions of civil society remained political.

Though the explicit nature of civil institutions was political, Marx carefully characterizes these institutions as decadent, fragmenting of human society, and as destructive to the general population. He then discusses the bourgeois revolution, a phenomenon which eliminated decadence by replacing the value structures to which decadence was bound:

> The political revolution which overthrew this power of the ruler, which made state affairs the affairs of the people, and the political state a matter of *general* concern, i.e., a real estate, necessarily shattered everything—estates, corporations, guilds, privileges—which expressed the separation of the people from community life. The political revolution therefore *abolished* the *political character of civil society*. It dissolved civil society into its basic elements, on the one hand *individuals*, and on the other hand the *material and cultural elements* which formed the life experience and the civil situation of these individuals . . . A *specific* activity and situation in life no longer had any but an individual significance.

The same forces created both the national state and the possibility of achieving success through individualist action. Marx explains, "Feudal society was dissolved into its basic element, *man*; but into egoistic man who was its real foundation." It was with this double-bladed knife that individualism cut its simultaneously cleansing and alienating swathe through the consciousness of early fifteenth century England.

But for the citizens of this historical moment, individualism as a basic value-structure had been seen before in history; it had been, and was still being, suffered within the religious memory. And, by 1400, citizens of an urban society were again beginning to act their contemporary profane role in accordance with individualist principles. The confusion between a Roman and a modern individualism, both for those who were living out the contradiction and for those who would later attempt to understand the implications of the contradiction, is great. I would like to try to clarify certain elements in this confused presentation of individualistic institutions at least preliminarily by suggesting the following schema:

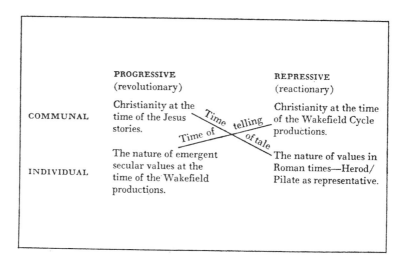

	PROGRESSIVE (revolutionary)	REPRESSIVE (reactionary)
COMMUNAL	Christianity at the time of the Jesus stories.	Christianity at the time of the Wakefield Cycle productions.
INDIVIDUAL	The nature of emergent secular values at the time of the Wakefield productions.	The nature of values in Roman times—Herod/Pilate as representative.

Hence late-medieval individualism must be seen doubly: from our historical and so, possibly, external perspective in the late twentieth century, as an initially progressive force the inherent contradictions of which are, at the time of the Cycle, merely incipient; and from the perspective of those in late-medieval England who feared losing their established powers, as a dangerous force which could take from them that which their predecessors had made or gained and retained, and which they would not lose. Handily, a wary church and political hierarchy could link the new individualism in its implicit manifestations with the worst excesses of its Roman counterpart.

This cannot be the place for cultural analysis of the society for whom the Wakefield plays were performed, much less for an economic examination of, for example, the Wakefield wool trade in the fifteenth century.[5] Nonetheless, to avoid speculating upon the nature of these audiences as if the plays existed in a documentary void would be to pervert not only their meaning but also their intention. By intention here I do not mean: Why were the plays performed? Answer: Because it was Corpus Christi Day. Rather, intention should refer to those deep-seated structures of thought which create social forms to satisfy both plural economic needs and the most widely felt human effect of those needs, psychological uncertainty.

For dramatic history the first question and in some ways the least obvious must be, Why theater in the first place? And, in the second place, How could a fourteenth century theater have been Christian in nature? The mystery cycles came under the protection of the very institution which had forbidden earlier presentation not only of profane drama but also of sacred materials on the grounds that the stageplay by its very essence was destructive to the morality of mankind. Between the *Quem Quaeritis Trope* and the Wakefield Cycle, more than four hundred years and much Christian ideology had passed by. But neither pure dramatic nor religious scholarship is very helpful in explaining the basic causes of the ideological development in the attitudes of the Church which allowed, in the fifteenth century, full-blown dramatic presentations to take place.[6] Here the purpose will be to attempt such an explanation in terms of what

can be learned of the social and economic needs of the
fifteenth century audience as those needs are elicited
from the Wakefield Cycle of plays.

The Social Circumstance of the Plays

The hypothesis which underlies this analysis, a hypothesis drawn from practical dramatic production and an
assumption essential to anything that follows, is this:
that all successful dramatic presentation is conceived by
the producers of a dramatic event with a specific audience range in mind. The successful play or plays will
always cater or pander to, or attack or challenge, or titillate or defend or support, or any combination of these,
the basic values of the audience. The producers, like the
integration propagandist, ignores the audience's value
structures to his peril.

Further, such a hypothesis contends that the authors
and the producers of the annual pageant in Wakefield
understood their audience full well; that they recognized
it as somewhat disparate in terms of its value system but
yet saw the continuum of that value system as lying
within a circumscribed and containable mainstream.
That is, the conscious progressives in the audience were
reasonably relaxed about a new individualism raising its
institutions in a variety of traditional areas and somewhat discomfited by the prevailing repression of the
older feudal institutions. The conscious conservatives
tended toward the previous, proven forms of governance
and social organization and looked on evolving individualism with considerable mistrust. And most members
of the audience, not bothering to separate out the old
from the new, took pleasure in both the satisfying spectacle and the human actions imitated, heightened, and/
or mocked on the stage. In this respect, most theater
audiences were and to a considerable extent remain similar. Therefore, from among the several relatively contemporary mystery cycles, I have chosen to deal with the

Wakefield pageants partly because they are the most easily accessible to modern readers, but more importantly because they represent the most varied forms of presentation.[7]

It is further important to note that the audiences of the late fourteenth century *needed* theater, or something like it, to satisfy a desire decreasingly catered to by the Church itself, a desire for meaningful and satisfying ritual, as such ritual grows out of and relates to daily experience. Vernacular sermonizing in the churches was an increasing phenomenon,[8] replacing an outworn Latin ritual the meaning of which was growing ever more obscure to congregations always further removed from the social/mystical source of the ritual forms. Sermonizing itself answered some individualistic needs—the direct relation between a man and his holy representative —but it did not satisfy the need for immediately experienced ritual, for a ritual comprehensible to an unlettered population. Vernacular rituals in the form of dramatic presentation were able to satisfy some of this demand. In addition, as Allardyce Nicoll has shown, the power of dramatic presentation was such that, despite its official suppression, it continued to flourish even between the fourth and tenth centuries.[9] This power, the Church at last realized, could be harnessed to its own ends. Two ideological circumstances are suggested by this ecclesiastical turnabout, two sides of the same coin: first, that audiences felt they needed greater contact with the largest elements of the universe, with the eternal and the infinite, than the Church was providing; and second, that the Church found itself once again employing its genius for survival by embracing yet one more popular indigenous institution, dramatic presentation. When popular drama could no longer be suppressed it had to be pre-empted, contained, and translated into a predominantly Christian idiom.

This process was certainly not part of a system of direct cause and effect. I do not wish to suggest that Rome gave orders to its lieutenants to infiltrate systematically all traveling satyr shows, or to undermine the organizers of Morris and Sword dances. Rather, a new consciousness, based materially among disgruntled congregants, was making itself felt to all levels of clergy; in order to speak directly to their several flocks, the proper idiom was necessary, and this idiom was best found amid the congregations to whom the Word should be addressed. At the possible extremes of presentational phenomena there were traditions: at one end a powerful source of ritual was still the church service itself; at the other, the mimetic end, mummery and Robin Hood players provided a continuing model for anarchy and foolery. But traditions, as much in a preliterate society as in any other, tend to contaminate and often to enrich each other. In the case of the evolving drama between the tenth and fourteenth centuries, this enrichment was itself penetrated, and so increasingly enriched, by content from Christian sources, sources which simultaneously imposed onto the resultant plays an ideology consistent with the values of those economic classes sufficiently powerful to stand on equal footing and to interact with the Church hierarchy itself. (In many cases, it must be noted, the ruling classes and the Church hierarchy were synonymous embodiments.)

The dominant late-feudal religious/economic ideology and its institutions embraced dramatic presentation and came to use theater as yet another tool for anesthetizing the increasing number of potential dissidents, urban dwellers beginning to grow disconnected from the dominant Christian hegemony. In this context, two groups of minimal ideological initiative can be examined as discrete units within a larger system: those who put the play together, and those specific groups that would comprise the audience. Like any audience, it ranged in consciousness, even in the provinces, along a political spectrum the extremes of which were determined by the social moment. This politically spectrated audience becomes important if it is granted that social conservatism and/or liberalism (and at the extremes, reactionism and radicalism) cease being abstractions and become a large element in the basis of immediate psychological response (cheering, laughing, booing, applauding; "What an awful play," "What a fine scene," "I feel asleep,") displayed by the members of the audience. Certainly the political and economic backdrops of a play, implicit and explicit, are not the sole causes of an audience's psychological response. But equally as certain, they form a large segment of that response, and as such must be catered to, or attacked, or whatever, by the production.

It can be said, then, that at the moment in history here in consideration, the moment of the Wakefield Cycle, the audience was comprised of a large body of people, some more caught up in a response to the pro- and/or anti-feudal and/or bourgeois material being presented dramatically; and some less caught up. The historical moment of the Wakefield Cycle is long, and so not static but evolving. And within that moment the plays too evolved—they were in 1350 different in production and intention from what they would be by 1420. The plays assisted in their small, once-a-year way in the ideological evolution of their audiences; the audiences came to demand more from the plays; the authors/producers of the plays complied; and the ruling classes which allowed the existence of these productions held the ideological reins.

A word about those who made the plays. Arguments over the name of the Wakefield Master, about his association with the strong nine-beat line, about the authorship of specific plays in the Cycle, these are in the end reductive, particularly if the plays did in fact evolve from earlier models. Instead, we can learn more about the plays themselves and how they functioned in their societies by expanding the concept of authorship to a disorganized kind of collection, one comprised of: the Wakefield Master and his school (itself a confused category); other playwrights; actors with ideas about how to make a scene work more smoothly; directors with a knowledge of stagecraft, and with a sense of where to cut a speech and where to improve a passage; transcribers who missed an addition or a deletion and/or added or changed a line to express what they felt to be their own wit; and the general impromptu mistakes and inspirations of the hundreds, even thousands of people involved over the years with the production of the plays. To assume that the productions happened, neatly and smoothly, true to script, year after year, is at very best naïve to the difference between individual poetic composition and (dis)organized dramatic presentation. The plays were successful precisely because they were the product of a plural and evolutionary authorship, able to address itself to the material needs of the changing audiences.[10]

Some interesting theorizing has been done on the relationship between the extant dramatic material and the actual play in contextual production. Hans-Jürgen Diller reminds us that "it is commonplace among historians of the drama that the medieval audience were much more interested in lively stage business than in polished dialogue,"[11] suggesting again that the play as read may be quite different from the play produced. A hiatus in the text, an obvious fault to the reader, might suggest an excellent transitional bit of stage business which elevated the play from adequate verse to fine drama. And, in a larger way, Wallace Johnson suggests that the Mak and Gill foolery of *The Second Shepherds' Play* may have its source in Christmas Saturnalia improvisations, that these were first superimposed onto and finally evolved into an integrated part of the whole play through several hands.[12] The sources for this kind of emendation would have been known to many members of a medieval audience, and the particular formal associationism in the play would add to audience pleasure. It was to the ideological advantage of the playwright(s) to use such emendation to their own ends, ends identifiable with those of the hegemony altogether.

But that these plays should be identifiable with hegemonic integration propaganda should in no way be taken to mean that the playwrights were the explicit tools of waning feudal ideology. The argument runs: because a certain Bible story is, as we all know, sacrosanct, the topics of the plays are completely dictated by tradition, and a playwright's imagination and talent are left no room to maneuver. And further: audiences come at the time of religious holidays to see religious spectacles, so that, from the perspective of the audiences, drama and local color are not only out of place but also undesirable. However, the last decade has provided a good deal of intelligent critical analysis and re-evaluative scholarship which demonstrates the limitations of such claims.[13] In addition, any knowledge or sense of dramatic creation, production, and presentation to an audience renders the suggestion of absolute clerical control absurd, and narrowly religious audience desires ludicrous. It therefore begins to become clear that, though on the superficial level the plays may depict a wide spectrum of political and social attitudes in order to capture and hold their audiences, on a more profound structural level the Wakefield Cycle demonstrates its own very clear ideology, and this ideology is essentially conservative.

The Ideology of the Plays

An audience sees the whole of a play in one of two primary ways: either as contemporaries of the play's creation, or as observers retrospective to the play and to its time. In the contemporary view, late medieval for the purposes of this discussion, the audience sees a play from within the ideology of its own cultural context, the largest part of which is so integral to daily life that there is no way for most in any audience (tutored nearly entirely or entirely in synchronic values) to appreciate the play against a historical background. The values of the play, the codes within a given scene, are rooted in the daily and usually unconscious practices and psychic structures of the audience. Simultaneously, the specific moments and passages of the play—the elements which cause the audience to recognize and react, and by which an audience decides if a play is good or bad, if it works or doesn't—these are also the daily details of contemporary life portrayed in that passage. Hence, *to a contemporary audience, the ideology of the play remains hidden* behind recognizable, and so normally unquestioned, detail. To render the ideology manifest would demand that a play's audience simultaneously render manifest the ideology of its own times, and virtually no member of an audience is, or was, ever either willing or able to do this. What *was*, for medieval and most other audiences, was *natural*. A Christian world was the best world. The other possibilities—paganism, or more immediately, the infidel and his visible embodiment, the whole of the Muslim scourge—were abhorrent alternatives. For example: in an appropriate threat, the Pilate of *The Conspiracy* swears against Jesus, "By Mohammed's blood so dear, / He shall cower at my command" (335). The anachronism speaks directly to the Wakefield audience, at this moment and throughout the pageant, and destroys for the audience any last vestige of the Pilate character's admirability: you cannot trust one who swears a Muslim oath. The audience need never question the immense oracular powers of such a Pilate. By his own oath he condemns himself. Infidels, whether Roman or Muslim, are despicable—and interchangeable.

In the retrospective view of a play an audience is capable of the overview necessary to place the play historically, and so able to make judgments: the play is dated; or, it holds up well over the years. But something is lost as well: there is most often little sense of the historical function of the play in and for its own time, because latter-day audiences are usually ignorant of the specific values and needs of the play's original (its contemporary) audiences. The extent to which a play wears well over the years is the extent to which a playwright or director chooses for the details he or she stresses material which transcends its merely momentary social connections, while at the same time keeping the details

away from such generalizations that they become
merely banal.

Full judgment of a play, therefore, comes best when
retrospection and a historical anthropology—useful for
ferreting out time-bound values, social patterns, political
and economic structures, and whatever else is buried by
time—are held together by a more synchronic psychological sense of human patterns of activity. If the Wakefield Cycle is examined as a medieval restatement of certain Bible stories, as primarily a religious event that took
place once a year, then both the intrinsic structured
meaning of the plays and their extrinsic human purposes
are obscured. The plays may attempt to pass themselves
off, often abetted by scholarly mediation which sees the
plays at their face value, as vehicles that portray eternal
Christian values; but this view of their purpose, both as
political and as artistic phenomena, is insufficient.

Instead, these plays must be seen as late-feudal articu-
lations of temporally bound beliefs and institutions only
secondarily touching on eternal themes. The Christianity
of the Cycle is partisan conservative, a Christianity profoundly caught up in the larger economic and political
values of a declining land-based society. The Wakefield
Cycle demonstrates once again the genius of Christianity
in making use of contemporary materials for a conservative statement as to the nature of men and women,
people in general, and therefore, of course, late-medieval
persons (in whose idiom and for whose pleasure the
plays are written), in order to retain control over the
largest possible number of people.[14] Some attention has
been paid, most convincingly by Eleanor Prosser, to the
English mystery plays' ability to hold and move an audience because the plays were convincing dramatically
(that is, the plays as, simultaneously, effective theater
and as translations of religious materials); for present
purposes it is important to ask what this concept, effective drama, meant to an audience in Wakefield.

To see the plays as religious events, the double exposition of their doctrine and the variations upon this doc-

trine suffices. To see the plays as theatrical events, an explication of dramatic structures and devices is necessary. Crudely put, the aesthetician need deal only with thematic content and dramatic form; but to see the plays as symptoms of changing social values, it is essential to examine the trappings which surround the stories—the local and contemporary color which transcends the Bible stories from which the plays have grown—in order to explain *why* these stories were translated into a dramatic form in the first place.

All that the God of the beginning of *The Annunciation* has made, he implies, is good. His fear of loss would not have been aroused unless there were a sense of external challenge: the Roman persecution of the true way at the time of the play, the onslaught of destructive (though perhaps attractive) individualism at the time of the telling. From God's perspective all of Christian feudalism—the religious and the political/economic hegemony intricately interwoven—having been if not made in heaven at least consecrated by the Church fathers, is good. To explore the dangers felt to be threatening such a feudalism it is necessary first to examine this good feudal life as the plays portray it; then to examine the challenge, also from the perspective of the plays; and finally, from a historical perspective available only from outside the plays, to evaluate the implicit ideological stance advanced by the Cycle.

The best elements of the traditional feudal values, though often proclaimed, are only occasionally portrayed. The exemplary Paterfamilias of *The Conspiracy* displays not only the generosity looked for in the perfect vassal, but also the open communality which had formed, in the time of Jesus, a radical departure from Roman hedonism. At the time of the Wakefield productions, such generous communality would have become decreasingly possible as a precept by which to live a daily existence. Paterfamilias, told by John and Peter that Jesus needs a large room wherein to hold the Passover feast, responds with no hesitation, "Sirs, he is welcome unto me, / And so is all his company; / With all my heart and all my will / Is he welcome to stay his fill" (341). After which, the character Paterfamilias disappears from the play; both in the content of his speech and in his function, he serves the play and his world as a self-effacing catalyst. From the perspective of a religious and economic system which prefers to see its flock as sheep in whom communality has deteriorated to passivity, Paterfamilias is the ideal congregant because he is controllable without expense of energy or thought; he is the totally integrated subject.

But rarely in the Cycle is it possible to find a purely "good" (passive) human being. Most often, when the traditions of communality are lauded, they are in fact depicted in dramatic tension: that is, a character in whom communality and individuality are mixed comes into conflict with pure villainy; and his opposition to villainous individuality moves him toward communal virtue. Villainy is clearest when it stands alone, as in Pilate's Machiavellian speech (Machiavellianism being the political equivalent of the intellectual Cartesian *cogito:* two forms of an individualism which, though not yet specifically labeled, are already close at hand).

I am he that may make or mar a man;
Myself if I it say as men of court now can;
Support a man today, tomorrow against him plan,
On both parts thus I play, and, feigning, fight in the
    van
Of right;
But all false indicators,
Courtmongers and jurors,
And all these false outriders,
Are welcome in my sight.   (*The Conspiracy*, 332)

Sister Nicholas Maltman[15] draws attention to Pilate's first speech in *The Scourging*, in which, in a similar manner, he says of himself,

I am full of subtlety,

Falsehood, guile and treachery;
Therefore I am named by clergy
As *mali actoris*.
For like on both sides of iron the hammer makes it
   plane,
So do I that have here the law in my keeping,
The right side to succor certain I am full fain,
If I may get thereby advantage of winning.
             (*The Scourging*, 373–374)

Sister Nicholas sees in "as *mali actoris*" a corruption of
the phrase *os malleatoris*, the mouth, or the mask, of the
hammer—that is, the mouthpiece or the imitator of the
devil. I would prefer to see both meanings so that the
phrase could function as a pun. In either case, Pilate
condemns himself yet further as a partisan for the side of
destructive, because totally self-seeking, individualism.
More importantly, there is in the speech an implicit
fear, on the part of the ideology which has put these
words in Pilate's mouth, that the values which lie in his
keeping are capable of destroying, if transplanted to the
present, such control as remains to the traditional power
networks. Where, in Roman times, a then traditional
individualism was the basis for decadent ideology, in the
fourteenth and fifteenth century it is Christian feudalism itself which has become decadent. Feudalism's rear
guard has become fearful of any new value system
which in its incipient stage might well be socially cleansing. Hence any impending renascence of individually
oriented values presents a profound threat to those des-
perately holding on even more precariously to the older
constructs of power. This incessant conflict between
new/old individual and old/new communal values is
basic to much dramatic tension—to what makes a good
play. Almost never, however, are either of these sets of
values to be found in pure expression; if the best of theater follows concrete material circumstances in the pattern of its tensions, then such a contamination of values
will be only natural.

The Christian hegemonies of the late Middle Ages, ever more mindful of buoying up crumbling institutions, could with little difficulty turn to inquisition, purification, and torture if these were necessary to remove suspected witches and devils from its congregation. When a so-called witch might be one who took it in his or her head to lead a life divergent from orthodox teaching— an adolescent in promiscuity, for example, enjoying individual pleasure; or a man successful very quickly in a small-scale capitalist venture, proving to all that he must have sold himself to the devil—such a one is usually acting out of beliefs experimentally individualistic. More complex is the extent to which a member of the feudal hierarchy goes beyond positive communal values (the mutually responsible protection of the whole community, for example), by himself attempting to impose excessive punishment on deviance, by himself acting in coercive individualistic fashion. Such a member of the hegemony may well be powerful because he has a sense of perspective: he sees in context the danger foreboded by a newly encroaching value system, and in order to withstand its onslaught turns around and deals with the proponents of the new system according to actions already based in the new values themselves. Herod, for example, acts out this double role. In *Herod the Great* he is nominally the representative of the Roman state (individualism) pushing its coercive defense of an outdated morality to the extreme of torture (archindividualism). But no Herod in his own time spoke and acted like the Herod of the play; this play's Herod is a recognizable feudal lord defending the personal, the individualist pleasures of his life against those who wish to do contemporary, that is communal, good. His tool is the same extreme of torture (archindividualism) utilized by the historical Herod. But he is the medieval despot dressed in biblical costume, and for the audience the association is made by recognizing the grave danger of archindividualism. In the context of the rest of the plays, the suggestion is constant that all embodiments of individualist thought are the same and, so, that any kind of individualism is dangerous to true feudal Christians.

In the play Herod speaks to his soldiers about his devices for treating the boy Jesus, who threatens his repressive rule. He begins with a general reaction:

> Stronger
> My anger, what devil me ails,
> To torment me with tales,
> That by god's dear nails,
> I'll stand it no longer!
> What the devil! How I blast for anger and spleen!
>
> (264)

And in speaking of three kings who brought the information about the boy, Herod continues,

> I tell you,
> A boy they said they sought,
> With offering that they brought;
> It moves my heart right nought
> To break his neck in two.
>
> . . . .
>
> Tortures untold they shall suffer each one,
> For ire,
> Such pains heard never man tell,
> Both furious and fell
> That Lucifer in hell,
> Their bones shall break entire.   (264)

But though Herod keeps his hands clean by attributing all imposed pain to Lucifer in hell, his servants and vassals know, and accede to the fact, that on earth it is Herod himself who acts the part of the sadistic torturer. Moments before Herod's entry, a messenger has told the audience,

> Drop down on your knees
> All that him sees,
> If him you displease,
> He will break every bone.

Here he comes now, I cry, of that lord I spake;
Fast before will I hie, me swiftly betake
To welcome him worshipfully, his mirth for to make,
As he is most worthy, and kneel for his sake
So low.

. . . .

Hail, lovely lord, anew; thy laws most firm are laid;
I have done what I could do . . .   (262)

Herod in his role as feudal lord extends himself in the
defense of his instituted power beyond constructive
Christian communal values; he is the power-hungry lord
run amuck. In terms of values, the confusion can again
be sorted out by differentiating between the time of the
telling and the time of the tale: the Roman Herod was
the exponent and the manager of extremes to which individualism could be taken in the defense of individualistic institutions; the late-medieval view of the Roman
Herod (of whom "none speak so well / as his cousin
Mohammed" [262]—again the destruction of historical
perspective) depicts him not as a practitioner of the extremes of an outmoded value system, but as one flirting
with the beginnings of a wholly new value system *in
order to keep himself in power*. In either case, demon
individualism is the culprit and, for the audience, a way
of life to be avoided.

The message should be clear: all forms of individualism are dangerous, whether on the part of the lowest in
the society, or on the part of the highest. Such propagandized egalitarianism at all levels of a hierarchic
communality is beguiling to an audience contemporary
with the play's production. The reformist landholder or
the successful bourgeois who would threaten a materialist clergy by denying it political authority would have to
be branded individualistic, hence pagan, hence Roman,
hence as everyone knows a great threat to the baby
Jesus—because individualistic, therefore in league with
the devil. Similarly, good Christians must withstand the
threat from below—not that soldiers or shepherds or the

rabble in general are any kind of a threat but they do grumble, and grumbling can be catching. "I have done what I could," says the messenger after Herod's entrance, but continues:

> ... and peace these people prayed;
> And much more thereto, openly displayed;
> But rumours rush through their mind till is made
> A vain boast.
> They carp of a king,
> They cease not such chattering.   (262)

In the time of the play, a king; in the time of the telling, a kind of dissatisfaction (outwardly prayers for peace) among the people that could become dangerous if the proper catalyst were found—a more convincing John Wycliffe, for example, whose Lollardry demanded such reforms supportive of individualism in English Roman Catholicism as would have thoroughly undercut the economic power of a Church coercively individualistic in support of a decaying communal system, had these reforms been universally accepted. Or a catalyst on the Continent such as John Huss, whose "heresies" in Bohemia broke open the ground on which a century later Luther could firmly stand. The conservative argument, complex and possibly unconvincing when presented discursively, found a compelling vehicle in the nonrational associations of theatrical production.

In most instances of lower class individualism the potentially liberating energies of the population at large have been perverted by their association with the larger powers of hegemonic individualism. The messenger who tells the audience about Herod's character is sufficiently anarchic to remain sympathetic until he comes under the spell and so the sway of his lord's actual presence. Thereupon fear of his master's individual wrath and destructive powers becomes the determining factor in the messenger's pose. Similarly, the infighting and quarreling on all grounds, all of them petty and personal, among the shepherds of *The First Shepherds' Play*, are dangerous; this the shepherds themselves are depicted as coming to recognize, because such squabbling threatens the serenity with which the birth of Christ must be greeted. And conversely, the impending birth of Christ as an all-pervading event is capable of rendering irrelevant the trivial bickering among men who think only of themselves and their immediate comforts.[16] The shepherds are easily penetrated by the proper mystical and passive side of communality, by that mysticism which becomes the dominant element at the end of the Cycle, particularly in *The Ascension of the Lord* and in *The Judgement*, as when Jesus in the former says, ". . . that man that may see me, / He sees my father full of might: / Trust thou not he dwells in me / And I in him if thou trust right?" (513). The antihistorical confusion and time-of-tale/time-of-telling is combined with this kind of mysticism, proto-Christian here, when the shepherds, about to lie down and go to sleep, agree not to brawl further; the third shepherd incants, again anachronistically,

> For fear and for fright by a cross be we blest,
> Christ's cross keep us right, east and west,
> In need,
> *Jesus onazorus*
> *Marcus, Andreus,*
> God be our speed. (199)

The soldiers who carry out Herod's orders to kill all male children, on the other hand, act with unrepentant selfish pleasure; in them the values of their masters have been more thoroughly internalized. In describing to Herod their success, his orders have become the soldiers' pleasure. The third, summing up the enthusiasm, says,

> Had ye seen how I fared, when I came among them!
> There was none that I spared, but laid on and dang
>   them!
> When they were so scared began I to bang them.
> I stood and I stared, no pity to hang them
> Had I. (275)

Herod swears ("By Mohammed's renown," naturally,) that they shall each have a maid to wed for their loyalty. They complain and ask for money instead; Herod agrees. The loyalty of a vassal has been reduced, from generosity and natural interaction between men sworn to protect and assist each other, down to a single economic transaction, that of paying off the murderers. As John Gardner points out, the medieval audience was well aware of the difference between a good vassal bound to a master out of common interest, and a bad vassal bound out of debt or payment.[17] The emphasis in each soldier's speech goes well beyond any point of explanation of the event. Rather it centers on the cleverness or the power or the extremity of each soldier's actions. Not only his deeds but also his telling of them has as its intent each narrator's desire to glorify himself in his own, in his compatriots, and finally in Herod's eyes.

That such individualism cannot, according to the values of the plays, ever lead to good becomes more blatant as the Cycle progresses. The soldiers only kill male children; the torturers of *The Talents* abuse the very body of Jesus on the cross with attitudes and actions based in values parallel to those of the soldiers. The First Torturer says,

> At Calvary when he hanged was,
> I spued and spat right in his face,
> When that it shone as any glass
> So seemly to my sight;
> But yet for all that fair thing
> I laughed at him in hating,
> Robbed him of his clothing,
> To me it was but right.　　(433–434)

Whatever the immediate (dramatic) psychological reason for this arrogance in the torturers, their pose can be seen as the masquerade for a guilt or an uncertainty or a fear or whatever its actor desires to show the character concealing both from himself and from his inter-

locutor. The psychological insight of the Wakefield
authors in a passage such as this is considerable.
Less psychological insight but greater catechismal
pedagogy is demonstrated in *The Pilgrims* when, unbeknown to them, Luke and Cleophas meet Jesus on the
road and Luke says of the crucifixion, "I wept for I was
so dismayed, / My grief was raw." Jesus' response,

> Ye fools, ye are not stable!
> Where is your wit, I say?
> Both bewildered and unable
> To reckon the right way,
> For believe it is no fable
> That has befallen this same day.   (428)

chides the two for thinking primarily of themselves and
their own grief instead of understanding the greater
implications of the death of the one who has died for all.
The playwright and his hegemonic sponsors enlist the
confusion between time-of-telling and time-of-tale to
support their warning against the destructive implications of individually based reason. The play depicts
Jesus as asking Luke to utilize a transcendent form of
religious/dramatic wit and, implicitly, to relate that wit
to mystical communality; thereby the dramatic and
ideological structures abet the narrative confusion.

The method of this confusion is complex and demands
an exploratory tangent. Three levels of consciousness in
dialectical interaction are implicit in the Jesus/Luke
exchange. Each level is discrete to the action of the
play's world. Simultaneously each is confusable with the
other levels. Such a mode of confusion has been essential
to the workings of the best bourgeois drama. It can be
utilized for the didactic purposes of the sponsor; or, in
less Machiavellian, more liberal and generous terms, for
the enjoyment of the audience. In their simplest forms,
the first level can be seen as pragmatic reason, based
here on sense perception, since Luke's eyes can tell him
what is. The second calls for a leap of faith to mystical
awareness of Jesus as the ritual embodiment of the per-

fect communal system. The third institutes a new form of pragmatism, pragmatism now in holy guise; within holy pragmatism each detail of thought and of activity leads directly and logically to the absolute.

The second level, only implicit in Jesus' words above, subordinates pragmatism of the first order to mystical awareness. In the passage Jesus asks the pilgrims for more than they can give, more since they have not yet transcended first-level pragmatism. They have not yet, that is, made that leap of faith which renders previous pragmatism both naïve and obsolete—and in the early fifteenth century, potentially dangerous because individualistic.

Once Luke and Cleophas attain this "higher" and more passive consciousness, they would then become capable of utilizing their wit, or reason, to ends demanded by a third, the "highest" kind of consciousness, that which participates in every way in a knowledge of the absolute. The trouble is that, for a mind insufficiently saturated with mystical belief, the achievement of the third level is impossible. An audience's (congregation's) hope for the potential attainment of this third state—which for Christian purposes can be labeled purity of the soul, or state of grace, or any euphemism for a religiously determined, socially fragmenting perfection—served as the hegemonic control lever over the audience, as a *deus ex machina* that was never allowed on the stage.

For dramatic purposes, the confusion between the first and third level of consciousness is the most important. It establishes the tension between the immediate rough state of audience impurity and the ultimate achievement of audience perfection. In *The Pilgrims*, the third level is only hinted at; later, in *The Ascension of the Lord*, Jesus mentions it directly and hints at the difficulty of achieving it in mortal days. Speaking to Philip of the heaven to which he is going, Jesus says, "In his house is many a place, / Which I go to prepare for you: / Ye shall all be filled with grace, / The holy ghost I shall send to you" (513). This grace, the ultimate carrot on the stick, is attainable only to those who believe, and then readily; but to come to Belief without first believing, this is impossible. In linear terms the circumstance is a complete paradox. But theater is not linear, and so adapts itself readily to the perverse dialectics of mysticism necessary to render the paradox acceptable.

And therein lies one of the major positive reasons for a theater sanctioned by the Church: dramatic presentation can portray powerful evidence of a clearly organized perception of nature without compromising itself to secular rationality. Theater, though a predominantly individualistic mode, hence a tool of rationalism for its creators to use, can have for its effect on an audience quite the opposite: simultaneity, dialectical presentation, ritual association, mystical involvement. In this way theatrical performance can itself serve as the vehicle that moves members of the audience from pragmatic immediacy to, and through, mystical consciousness to the third level, on which experience is directly associated with Belief.

The element that makes these plays "work" is an audience titillation based on confusion between the first and third levels, a confusion that results in a sense of actually being in physical touch with the absolute. But for purposes of political control the second level of consciousness is the most important. When the playwright can successfully depict the concept of reason contributing to passive grace (Jesus: "ye shall be filled," etc.), then positive and potentially cleansing individual reason (in the time of the telling) has been pre-empted, and the traditional institutions can remain unquestioned and unattacked. The perfect late-medieval state, from the perspective of hegemonic control, is the passive and so unchanging community. Communality of the sort determined by feudal Christianity would, it was hoped, restore the audience and the community to an apparent and unchanging utopia, one characterized by peace, that is, lack of conflict. Such peace avoids any changing distribution of wealth and power and becomes the image of an Eden frozen in colorful illumination. But the problem was that by the beginning of the fifteenth century the existence of such an ideal lay inscribed only in the romanticized and propagandized memory, mislabeled "history", of a conservative economic base, clergy and nobility, which tried to hearken back to a past that had never been, to use the sense of a lost golden age as the basis for control over its vassals, its congregations, and more specifically here, its audience. It was a simple matter, dramatically, to combine (from the perspective of the time of the tale) the lost utopic phenomenon (now set in the future) with the double implication of the future itself: after the death of Jesus, and after the time of the playing of the death of Jesus. A leap on the part of the audience from the first to the second level of consciousness, from pragmatic reason to ritual awareness of Jesus as the embodiment of the absolute, was far simpler on a stage than it was even in the cathedral. After all, there *was* a Jesus on the stage, a visual reminder of a known truth. Of course, everyone *knew* it was only an actor playing Jesus; but in the same way, everyone knew also that the embodiment of the spirit of Jesus was on the stage, right there in front of them. Whatever the details of the dramatic convention for accepting the actor as the character he is playing, every member of the audience gives some level of credence to the events on the stage (or else walks out, or goes away, or falls asleep). The perpetrators of an ideology have succeeded in harnessing such an audience's credence to its own ends when the audience has accepted the ideology along with, and because of, the convention. And equally important, the identification of the form of acceptance (an audience is passive) with the response demanded by the ideological message (a society should be passive) helps the audience make the leap to the second level of consciousness, that of passive awareness. At the moment of viewing the play, they are already partway there.

But *only* partway, and this qualification keeps dramatic (representationally narrative) art from becoming mechanical: for a successful play is not an ideological sermon or lecture or statement. It *can be suffused* with ideology, and so serve its sponsors. Implicit and embodied values are far more flexible than values blatantly exposed; the wise hegemonic agent will only suggest, though repeatedly, his message. When a play tries to be a sermon, the ideology usually kills its vehicle. This brings back the colloquy between Jesus and the pilgrims: even those who love Jesus—whether the pilgrims, or those in the audience who are already partway *to* the beliefs called for by the sponsors, or only partway *from* these beliefs and so still savable—are subject to demon individualism, to that value source which at its extreme denies the possibility of transcending pragmatic reason. The pilgrims must purge themselves of the demon; those in the audience must move totally into the second level of consciousness, the passive acceptance of the teachings of the Church. The audience is told, implicitly, that they are luckier than the pilgrims, for they have the whole Church as their guide, while Luke and Cleophas have only the word of Jesus, in whose immortality they have difficulty believing. The audience has the advantage of a perspective of more than thirteen additional centuries; such a perspective, which has proven Luke and Cleophas wrong, is also able to render the image of passive consciousness (and, thereby, acceptance of waning Christian feudalism) desirable.

It is of course impossible, in the experience of a play, to separate out the dramatic effect of the tension between the first and third levels of consciousness on the one hand, and on the other the political demands implicit on the second level. The simultaneity of levels gives the audience pleasure, their interaction gives the play its meaning, and their repressive dialectics contains the basic ideology of its sponsors.

The continuum of kinds of dramatic conflict is greater in *The Second Shepherds' Play* than in any other single unit in the Cycle, but the kinds of oppositions it contains are found throughout the other plays. At the one extreme of this continuum is the basic binary opposition, between anti-Christianity and Belief, which cannot be reconciled. At the other end is the movement from a refusal to believe, through doubt, to faith—that process of movement which ultimately leads, sometimes with dramatic sleight of hand, to the third level. In *The Ascension of the Lord*, for example, at the point where the extant play stops—it lacks in the manuscript the final twelve leaves—Mary tells the Apostles that they must disseminate the information about Jesus' ascent: "To the whole city these tidings disclose, / Tell the words of my son in world most wise: / Bid them in him their belief to repose, / *Or else* be they damned as men full of vice" (519, my italics). This is the complete either/or situation: he who does not believe is damned. There are few either/or situations in the Cycle. This relative absence is consistent with a desire on the part of the sponsors to bring about a change in the mental set of the audience by "bringing it back" to the hegemonic concept of an earlier purer age. Even Mary's binary opposition contains within it a way out, since there is no time limit set on an acceptance by the people of Jerusalem of a belief in Jesus' ascension.

Most of the plays are less blatant in stating the necessity to move from arrogance to belief. Usually there is less exposition and more demonstration. In perhaps the most famous case, that of Thomas of India in the play bearing his name, the movement to belief is thematic, and is presented doubly. First Mary announces Jesus' ascension; ten Apostles disbelieve, more willing to accept ghosts and spirits than Mary's information, but they are quickly brought round to orthodoxy.[18] Then Thomas appears and must face what is now a majority of believers. Though his doubt is strong because more profound than that of the Apostles—"If that I proud as peacock go, my heart is full of care" (495)—he comes to shed tears, the necessary sign of repentance in the proud. For both vanity and a heart full of care are symptoms of the pride of

individualism in that both keep their bearer from overcoming doubt and thereby from coming into faith. Both
pride and an uncertain spirit are symptoms of doubt; any
conflict between the two is, from a Christian communal
perspective, irrelevant and therefore dangerous. Both are
symptoms of the doubting individual and both portray
the individual as conceiving of himself in his selfish
inner suffering as more important than the faith he has
not achieved. The path to faith is the ideological center
of Christian life; the conflict between various forms of
selfishness, on the other hand, centers on doubt and
attempts either to make a virtue of anti-Christian weakness or to hide this weakness under falsehood and feigned
superiority. To portray the selfish conflict in Thomas,
and then to bring it to conclusion by transcending it,
makes the Christian point.

Simultaneously the portrayal takes into consideration
the two levels of audience reason with which the aesthetic elements of the pageant are playing; and pragmatic rationalism, conflicting with the "wit" (lacking in
Luke and Cleophas) which leads to a "knowledge" of
Jesus' immortality,[19] provides the tension for Thomas'
play as well. To the extent that the audience is a momentary community, sharing the experience of the play (and
more: for most presumably came to the play from within
the city of, or from just outside, Wakefield), they are as
a group already potentially engaged in the leap of acceptance which Thomas, when he enters the play, has
not yet made. And conversely, to the extent that they
have themselves not completed the leap to faith, Thomas
is their representative. Each person in the audience must
go separately the rest of the way to faith: the first part
was merely the easiest.

The play, as noted earlier, itself is constructed on this
bipartite model: first the Apostles appear and are easily
moved; then Thomas begins his pilgrimage to faith, and
he alone needs great convincing. Again the point is carefully insinuated: the individual is more dangerous; the
group can be moved to understanding. Or, seen from the

perspective of the integration propagandist, the mass mind, nonanalytical and undifferentiated, is more easily controlled. When at the end of the play Thomas begs mercy from Jesus, Jesus makes it clear that Thomas must shed his individualism and all that it implies. Mourning for the dead Jesus is far from throwing off one's selfishness. Rather, mourning is the very opposite; mourning allows one to feel sorry for oneself because now the master or the beloved or the habit is dead, hence no longer available for easy faith or comfort.

Some have transcended this doubt without knowing it. In *The Judgement* the Good Souls have difficulty understanding why they are in fact good, especially if good is defined as doing good works for Jesus himself. Jesus tells them, "My blessed bairns, I shall you say / What time these deeds were to me done; / When any that need had night or day, / Asked of your help and had it soon; / Your free heart said them never nay, / Early nor late, midnight, nor noon, . . ." (537). To do good for any who is downtrodden is to do good for Jesus. Not understanding this means that the Good Souls are still partially caught up in an intellectual pragmatic reason born of individualism. In their actions, however, they have made the total leap by which experience leads logically to faith; indeed, all experience is a symptom of faith. The Souls are good despite the evils that control values on earth.

The Cycle also explores the method by which one may move consciously from doubt to faith: by acting out the basis of faith *as if one believed*. In *The Ascension of the Lord* Jesus tells the gathered company,

Magdalene spoke my will, that I was risen, ye did but scold
Her, trusting not for good or ill the truth as she it told.
Such harms in hearts ye hold, unsteadfast in your prizing,
To believe none were ye bold, who bore witness of my rising;

Therefore ye shall go teach in all this world so wide,
And to all the people preach who baptism will abide.

(512)

Again, action brings faith; mourning merely regenerates
itself. The gathered apostles sustain Jesus' model by depicting their miraculous acceptance of the second level
of consciousness before the very eyes of the audience:
now they don't believe, now they do. Some may call such
instantaneous transition bad theater, because it appears
insufficiently motivated. But precisely here the linear
causality which suffuses too much of post-Isben drama
and dramatic production may not be used as the standard
for a judgment of this theatrical magic (*magic* for want
of a better word): the whole purpose of presenting ideology through dramatic rather than sermonized form is
to bring about the same instantaneous leap of faith in the
audience which the audience can see depicted and find
quite normal on the stage. This pedagogic device makes
use of the same technique which supports the confusion
between Jesus on the stage and the actor who plays Jesus:
of course no leap of faith took place because it was only
a piece of religious history that was acted out, thinks the
doubter; but yet the audience *saw* things as different
after the shift to belief had taken place.

Again, only a depictive and dialectical narrative form
can gain from an audience the necessary suspension of
doubt which allows the playwright to slide his argument
under the senses and into the mind. If it is done well and
the audience is sympathetic or only minimally antipathetic, audience members can find themselves believing
in the action before they know why. It is the circumstance Joseph of *The Annunciation* finds himself in when
he discovers Mary's pregnancy: "With her I can no
longer be," he says, "I rue that ever we met" (181). But
in his own way he is treated to a metaplaylet, the appearance of the archangel Gabriel who, while Joseph
may gasp in surprise, tells Joseph to accept what has happened: "Meek and obedient look thou be" (184). If one

is visited by a visible God, acceptance of faith would be the only possible religious reaction. Gabriel the archangel is powerful enough a figure to bring Joseph to the necessary second level of Christian consciousness, rendering him passive in his response to and subsequent acceptance of Mary's pregnancy. The larger political implications of these dramatic sleights of hand are considerable. The suggestion of such implications should not, however, be understood as a positivist attempt to relate specific plays to specific political events; rather, the issue here is the relationship between the ideological structure of the plays and the evolving nature of those values upon which political, social, and economic institutions are organized.

The largest evolution of values was the beginning of a move away from purely land-oriented feudal Christian communality toward non- (or even anti-) Christian, capital- and urban-oriented, individualism. In this context progress, for the good or bad, meant an awareness and an acceptance of the first symptoms of the new individualism and of their implications; and conversely, a decreasing trust or acceptance of institutions based on values predominantly communal. Conservatism meant both an avoidance of such values as denied the superiority of traditional communal life, and a defense of the medieval tradition; together with these the conservative would also engage in constant combat against the increasing acceptance by others of economic and even interpersonal institutions founded on individual values. The values of the Wakefield Cycle are based in this latter conservative complex.

The ideological demands made by the several plays' implicit values stand in considerable conflict with certain Christian narratives portrayed by the stories of the plays themselves. The repeated contradictions of a play's values set against the story the play tells help make it possible to elucidate the political implications of the Cycle as a whole. Central to the contradictions is this paradox: the strength of Christianity, and the element which from its earliest days was basic to its popular success, was its broad historical and synchronic perspective, its ability to see beyond marginal choices, initially those offered up from within Roman individualism. This perspective, once Christianity's greatest strength, is celebrated in the Cycle because the collectivized values of early Christianity are, at least in their outer propagandizable forms, still consistent with the values of the hegemony responsible for the telling of the tale fourteen hundred years later.

But the social/political *function* of a communal value system was very different after these fourteen centuries. At the time of the tale communal values created innovative institutions; at the time of the telling they supported old, drained, no longer needed institutions. Hence, the ability of Christianity to see its function within the largest possible perspective had, over the years, been lost (a not unusual circumstance when any neophyte group, the largest as well as the smallest, political or religious, comes to power). Christianity was no longer able to see, beyond the limited possibilities for human activity it itself had codified as natural law, choices within the ever-narrowing margin of communality. This is the other side of the audience's problem in dealing with the character of Thomas: when its antipathy is too great to allow the dramatist to get away with his "magic," his depiction of Thomas' leap to faith, then a member of the audience can say of the play that it does not work, that in fact it is a bad play. Such a statement would then clearly be bound to the political values of that member of the audience; what was successful dramatically in 1375 simply may not work any more in 1425.

So, though the Cycle refuses to allow, in the largest sense, the subsequent social generation to function freely, at least one play establishes the danger of a society or a leader that refuses, on the multi-individual level, life to the next generation. Herod commands that all male children in Bethlehem be killed, indiscriminately: "All male children ye slay, and lords, ye shall be stout, / That be

but two this day, and leave of all that rout / No child me
to dismay that lies in swaddling clout, / I warn you"
(270). The play next depicts three soldiers killing, separately, three male children of three mothers. One murder
would be an individual death; two would generalize the
murdering; three raises it to the necessary level of the
ritual murder of the next generation, rendering its horror far greater because now Death rather than deaths
threaten the community.

But the ongoing, if unregenerated, existence, at the
time of the telling, of Christianity itself proves the impossibility of destroying organic evolution toward a better human circumstance, symbolized religiously by the
successful flight of the baby Jesus and his parents; from
its earliest days Christianity integrated the dialectical
myth of History into its development (though not into
its dogma). Implicit in the myth of History is the ame-
liorative evolution of mankind despite the most thorough
efforts of repressive society. In the time of the tale Herod
as representative of Roman individualism acts the repressive role. By the time of the telling the repressive force
was played by hegemonic Christianity.

The Second Shepherds' Play

Herbert Marcuse explains that political control, wrested
from one generation by the subsequent, is a normal condition. This is the social Oedipal process. In the best of
times there is a balance between the values and functions
of the two generations; at extreme times, the two, or
those retaining power unnaturally and those out of
power but with all natural and organic right to it, are
in constant conflict. This duality, the generational interaction and/or the conflict between generations, is valid
for both the individual and the social circumstance:

> . . . the determining childhood experiences are linked
> with the experiences of the species—that the individ-

ual lives the universal fate of mankind. The past defines the present because mankind has not yet mastered its own history. To Freud, the universal fate is in the instinctual drives, but they are themselves subject to historical "modifications." At their beginning is the experience of domination, symbolized by the primal father—the extreme Oedipus situation.

But the circumstance is more complicated:

> In the Oedipus situation, the primal situation recurs under circumstances which from the beginning assure the lasting triumph of the father. But they also assure the life of the son and his future ability to take the father's place. How did civilization achieve this compromise?[20]

Marcuse's work grapples with civilization's question; here it is sufficient to suggest that the Wakefield playwright opted neither to seek the perspective necessary to cope with the evolution of values in his own time nor to deal progressively with the dramatic compromise or the dialectics which might have resulted from it. Instead he decided, though not necessarily consciously, to defend only one element in the social Oedipal pattern, the father figure—the powers of tradition, of the established feudal hierarchy and the dominant clergy. The threats from below, from the new generation and its potential power-base in the values of individualism, these were either ignored or condemned.

The opening lines of the Judas play suggest the abhorrence of the literalized Oedipal situation—the greatest traitor is characterized as having committed the greatest crime, even before his betrayal of Jesus Christ. Judas' first words are: "Alas, alas, and welaway! / Accursed caitiff I have been ay; / I slew my father, and after lay / With my mother; / And later, falsely, did betray / My own master" (390). He continues by providing an intendedly shocking account of his miserable past life. Because the play in manuscript is incomplete, to determine and state absolutely how the Judas story relates to the whole Cycle is impossible. But an explanation of the danger to established institutions that results if the social Oedipal process is allowed to function normally, progressively, was at least partly dealt with by the playwright; in the character of Judas the social process was transferred to the personal level. That the Wakefield master and his colleagues would have consciously associated, in abstract let alone labeled fashion, the Oedipus story with the larger social pattern to which it is parallel is doubtful. But the plays themselves show on the part of those who wrote the script an awareness of both these phenomena. It is also clear that the plays attempt to assist in curbing the direction in which the shift in social values was evolving. Though I have been calling that shift progressive, the Cycle's sponsors would have seen the social movement toward individualism as a pattern of decay and deterioration, a return to Roman paganism or worse, and so condemned it. Conversely, and from the advantage of a twentieth century perspective, it is now possible to speak of any hegemonic attempts in the fifteenth century to hold onto traditional communal values as decadent.

This forms an additional apparent paradox when dealing with the place of the Wakefield Cycle in dramatic history: here is a vibrant new form for the presentation of human experience which defends values already decadent in its own times. It is out of fear of this contradiction that *The Second Shepherds' Play* is usually granted the label "best" among the plays of the Cycle; it presents to modern critics, readers, and audiences the *least* contradiction between the new form of the Cycle and the material the play presents.

Bourgeois criticism is often uncomfortable when having to speak of the Cycle in hermetic terms for it is difficult to say much good of it. *The Second Shepherds' Play* is often discussed as the imperfect attempt of the playwright to shake off the vice-hold of the Church. But the pleasure of the play, in terms of the satisfaction it gives the audience, should not be expressed in the begrudging context of pure aesthetic criticism. To avoid the political implications, the open expression of class identification and conflict, is to miss entirely the high dramatic qualities of the action. The Wakefield playwright presents the play in three parts. First, the shepherds complain of their fate in highly social/political and economic terms: they are taken advantage of by their masters, and they are alienated from their wives and families by virtue of lonely nighttime duties. Their irritation takes the form of a discourse that ranges from ironic kidding to serious argument—a marginal attempt to show their own freedom within externally imposed confines. The second part of the play, the story of Mak, introduces drollery into this otherwise dismal life. Mak steals, and commentators generally find his exploits funny; it is important to recognize that much of the humor grows out of the relief an audience experiences when it sees the villain, the feudal lord and economic master, debunked by the play's poorest and most sympathetic character. In short, the play shows a society in which it is necessary for a man to become a thief in order to continue, physically, to survive: even in this protobourgeois play the circumstance indicts the society at least as much as it condemns the thief. So it is only appropriate from the perspective of the Cycle's sponsors that Mak be forced to give up the sheep after he and his wife have hidden it in the cradle and pretended it was a child. The three shepherds, economically and humanly alienated from their feudal lord, nonetheless are self-pressed to act as their lord's agents. The supposed child in the cradle then becomes the device linking the first three-quarters of the play to its conclusion, the birth of the real child, the nativity of Jesus, on the other side of the hill.

Slowly the audience comes to the awareness, consciously or intuitively, that the play deals with a class of human beings who are socially and psychologically repressed—shepherds in the time of the play, shepherds or tenant farmers or any oppressed groups including small bourgeois tradesmen and industrial crafts workers represented in the audience at the time of the telling. The play begins with pure exposition, the First Shepherd bemoaning his fate as he stands watching the sheep out in the bitter cold. He explains to the audience his relationship to his lord:

> We simple shepherds that walk on the moor,
> Are soon by richer hands thrust out of door;
> . . . .
> We are so lamed,
> Overtaxed and maimed,
> And cruelly tamed,
> By our gentlemen foe.

> Thus they rob us of our rest, may ill-luck them harry!
> These proud men are our pest, they make the plough
> tarry.
> What men say is for the best, we find it contrary:
> Thus are ploughmen oppressed, no hope now to carry
> Alive.
> Thus hold they us under,
> Thus bring us into blunder;
> It were great wonder,
> If ever we should thrive. (207–208)

As a statement of the symptoms of class struggle the passage could not have been worded more explicitly by any proletarian theorist; in *The Second Shepherds' Play* it is only the first of many passages that explore the implications of class antagonism, structurally as well as in image. The lord is characterized as "a swain, a proud peacock" (208), an image Thomas of India will later use of himself. The psychological relationship between the shepherd and his lord, and its economic basis, is equivalent to that between the messenger and Herod in the sixteenth play of the Cycle, the messenger hating Herod while hailing him as "lovely lord" (262). Facing the sum of aristocratic oppression, the First Shepherd knows the minimal human comfort of his place, and adds to the above words, "I were better be dead, / Than once say him nay." Yet he continues to cling to life in the only way he can; since he is the slave of the system that dominates, he can turn only to himself when he needs a trusted interlocutor.

In these early rumblings of the *cogito*, the shepherd works out in language the nature of his situation. On the most basic (the immediate dramatic) levels, his complaints about the unfairness of the universe make it easier to live within it—he labels the thing and so establishes the beginnings of control over it. "It does me good," he says, "as I walk this on my own, / Of this world for to talk, and so make my moan" (208). On the political level the implications of such a speech are broad: a need for the expression of internal activity begins to explain the emergence of social institutions based on individual values, institutions founded in order to respond to individual internal demands unanswered either by personal or by social circumstance. In more practical terms this means that all discourse (which here follows the monologue quickly, for both dramatic and political reasons) will be reduced to complaining, grumbling, and possibly, when unchecked, even anger and rebellion.

All personal relationships in this play are negative. The shepherds' fellowship is based on each one's condemnation of the others; misery does indeed prefer the company of misery. Even family relationships are undermined. Instead of the home as a center for the best that communality has to offer, one's hearth and the women who tend it are condemned as yet one more burden the poor (men) must suffer—quite opposite to the trust finally given another woman, Mary Magdalene, when all at last believe that Jesus has risen. Communal faith is not possible until *after* the arrival of Jesus, and *The Second Shepherds' Play* will end on this note. The shepherds are anticonnubial; men suffer in wedlock: "But young men a-wooing, on God be your thought," the Second Shepherd warns his compatriots in the audience. "Be

well warned of wedding, and think ere you're taught, /
'Had I known' is a thing too lately you're taught; /
Much bitter mourning has wedding home brought"
(210). In its implications much more than a diatribe
against marriage, this profoundly individualistic statement carried to its logical consequence would undermine
all communal elements in the social order. It would in
fact go far toward eliminating the next generation. But
though the shepherds understand their private miseries
in terms of social oppression, they do not attempt to
seek out the implications of their complaints and thereby
change their lot. Their untranscended grumbling leads
nowhere, and the play's hegemonically contrived values
will ultimately reward their passivity.

When the unrebellious lower classes refuse to take
action against the aristocracy, they become fodder to
feudalism and the social Oedipal project has failed. The
great potential strength of the shepherd class lies in the
dawning of their realization that each man is a unique
individual, as equally worthy of warmth, food, and material pleasures as is the aristocracy. But the shepherds
(in the time of the telling of the story) fail to become
conscious of the strength of mutual individualism; they
still accept the integration propaganda of the dominant
classes, here principally the Church, that every form of
individualism is evil and will keep its perpetrators from
heaven, from all subsequent nonmaterial rewards—the
only rewards for which the poor are even in contention.

Yet the shepherds are strong and sympathetic as characters. In so depicting them, the Wakefield Master is
beginning to play with ideological fire. The (hell-)fire
of pleasure is titillating, especially to audiences and commentators caught in a basic bourgeois contradiction, the
mutual exclusivity of pleasure and goodness. But titillation[21] is not progressive. Rather, while it challenges
standards which audiences, and societies, are beginning
implicitly to find dubious, it simultaneously undercuts
such challenges because it undermines an audience
member's courage to call these standards into question

out loud, and so to examine and subsequently to reject
them. Titillation by fire makes good theater and bad
progressive politics. Titillation is a supreme form of integration propaganda. Though it can serve as the initial
instigation for the negating elements in dialectic process,
alone it is never more than the suggestion, liberal in
nature, that at a more serious moment someone, some-
where (but not the commentator, not here, not now),
should take a look at why the titillation brings on the
pleasures of discomfort in the mind of a collaborative
audience. This is not to say that moments of titillation
will not exist in a theater that serves progressive ends.
Rather, when the political citizen has finished enjoying
the dramatic elements of a titillating play, she or he
might move on to analyze the social contradictions which
made the moment titillating (politically undermined by
dramatic art) and attempt to resolve those contradictions. But such analysis would be possible only from an
audience that was conscious previously and did not need
the play as an instrument of assistance toward becoming
conscious of the implicitly depicted issues.

An audience member may try to resolve the depicted
contradictions unless he or she is defeated by the whole
of the play itself—unless the playwright, knowing how
to titillate, how to raise all expectations, then disarms
the audience of its potential tools of analysis. So it is here.
If the weaponry for the elimination of social oppression
(in the time of the telling) is founded in individual
values, it is the job of the Wakefield playwright and his
sponsors to undercut that individualism before it can become attractive. Hence the first part of the play, the exposition from the shepherds as they grumble against
their lord in a manner so contemporary as to make their
audience aware from personal experience that the plight
of the shepherds closely overlaps their own, is undercut
by the second part, the Mak story, which depicts a peasant gone wrong, a peasant who would actually steal from
the established order. And it is within the Mak section
that the three shepherds, earlier the potential source for

social ferment, turn about and become the supporters of their own hated lord. They turn on Mak because *Mak has pushed their grumbling to its necessary conclusion*: if the lord is economically destructive, he no longer has such rights as the communal values of ideal feudal society would grant him. In truly communal fashion, and certainly in traditional Christian rhetoric, his properties would again become common property. In terms of the new individualism, each man has rights to this common property. In either circumstance, Mak's appropriation of the sheep is both consistent and just, and the three shepherds are left holding the contradictions.

The Wakefield playwright has attempted to present Mak as the embodiment of all the negative qualities of individualism, as the destroyer of communal harmony; it is likely he succeeded in this attempt only for the conservative factions in the audience. For the largest part of the audience, the middle-of-the-road section, Mak is political titillation pushed to its extreme. One step further would demand the question that could only be answered within the totality of political, economic, and social consciousness: How does one alleviate persecution and oppression? By overthrowing those who control the land and with it the economic basis for oppressive power.

But instead of one step forward, the Wakefield playwright takes three steps back. The shepherds are rewarded for their loyalty to the old communality; they alone and not Mak are given the privilege of basking in the glory of the baby Jesus and they alone are loosened from their material repression. "May he keep you from woe," Mary tells them, "I shall pray him do so." To which the First Shepherd responds, "What grace we have found," and the Second, "Come, now are we unbound" (234). So the question of alleviating oppression and persecution is answered not within a progressive consciousness, but finally within the reactionary elements of Christian tradition: one must return to the most glorious and perfect moment in Christian history—the most glorious because then all history (the time of Christian institutions) still lay ahead, the most perfect because as yet unmarred by concrete history. The fear that nothing lies ahead demands a retrospective and reevaluative vision. To a hegemony whose values function only within the myth of Science, reevaluation could only have undermined the complete economic basis for the material pleasures of existence, and the Church was not an anarchist institution.

A movement in history onward to communality is completely self-consistent aesthetically—that is, from within the context of the play, from the time of the tale. The same movement is absolutely inconsistent for the political play, the play in relation to its audience at the time of the telling. To that part of the audience capable of intellectually throwing itself into the action of the play, the lesson is successful, convincing all that Christian ways were in danger of being lost, that they must be supported. For the middle-of-the-road and the progressive members of the audience, as they moved on to the next wagon to watch *The Offering of the Magi*, the play could have aroused reactions ranging from a shrug of the shoulders and a superficial "maybe" to the considerable dissatisfaction of "things just don't work like that."

The question, then, of why the Wakefield playwright, having set up the first three-fourths of *The Second Shepherds' Play* as antihegemonic drama, should then turn about and undercut it, could be answered in one of two ways. Possibly (1) he was himself a serious social critic who, if allowed free rein, could have and well might have written progressive plays. Clearly he was addressing himself to the local audience. He has a general awareness of himself as playwright. The Cycle is sprinkled with dramatic metacommentary: Mak's wife says, when Mak tells her to pretend the stolen sheep is the child to which she has just given birth, "This is a cunning play and well cast" (219). His careful use of anachronisms (he was far too clever to make the mistake of having his shepherds exclaim or curse in the name of Christ *before* Christ's birth)[22] is a symptom of his knowledge both of the role he is playing and of the audience he is writing for. Or (2) he was simply an excellent dramatist without a conscious ideology, who knew how to capture and to hold an audience's imagination long enough for him to make his point, the traditional late-feudal Christian point.

If *The Second Shepherds' Play* existed in a void, if the rest of the Cycle were not mostly extant, it would be far more difficult to answer the question, how, politically, did this play function? But if we assume a consistency of intention between this play and the rest of the Cycle, the political meaning of both becomes a great deal clearer. It must be underlined again that consistency of intention does not preclude the possibility of contradiction: often, in fact, the voice attempting to be consistent within a timeworn, valueworn aesthetic gets so caught up by the consistency of intention it is defending that it portrays its contradictions with a wild unconscious glee. Much of the audience's political pleasure is then born of those tensions resulting from the attempt to keep a consistent cover on the play's material contradictions. To the extent that *The Second Shepherds' Play* is a situation comedy, à la Plautus or Molière, the contradictions prove humorous as they appear in the *content*: Mak pretending the sheep is a baby, his wife pretending she is still weak from her lying-in. But the deeper tension, especially of the first part of the play, and its political meaning grow out of the impossibility of reconciliation between the problems of the shepherds and the solution the play presents: politically the play's ending—salvation for these particular shepherds, with their fourteenth century attributes, through the birth and subsequent martyrdom of Jesus— is ridiculous. The attempts to make it less ludicrous— overstressing the shepherds' new-found freedom, letting them exit at the very end by singing "a glad sound" (234)—may well have seemed, to a progressive audience especially, at best embarrassing, but more likely foolish and laughable.

This is not to say that the play's ending comes out of

nowhere. The playwright is very careful to foreshadow
a psychological basis for the easy acceptance, on the part
of the shepherds, of passive (nongrumbling) Christian
communality. Not only are they cowards politically in
their defense of the property of a lord whom they hate,
they are also to some extent generous, if not to each other
then at least to the next generation: the Third Shepherd
is even willing to give an offering to Mak's "child." And
the language too prepares the audience for the shepherds'
suffusion within Christian ritual; the verses become far
more regular, the speeches far less gruff, after the appearance of the angel. Dramatically, the playwright and
his followers knew their devices.

Integration Propaganda in the Cycle

Devices similar to those in *The Second Shepherds' Play*
abound throughout the Cycle. The most predominant
among them are the two most opposed: the individual-
ized, sympathetic, and immediately recognizable character; and the ritually repeated informational liturgy
which becomes the basis of the Christian myth as the
Cycle presents it. The torturers in *The Talents*, for example, are, despite their roles, attractive churls who speak
some of the most elegantly colloquial lines in the Cycle.
The Second says,

> By leaps and bounds I needs must flit,
> As though I now had lost my wit:
> My breeches I had almost shit,
> So great was my delay.

And the Third develops the scatological mood:

> Out, alas! how do ye crones,
> Haste have I made to break my bones!
> I have burst both my bullock stones,
> So fast I hurried hither.

That they have just arrived from the scene of the crucifixion, that they have spat on the face of Jesus on the cross, that they have stolen his clothes, this in no way diminishes their attractiveness *as characters*. The message remains clear, however: rough-hewn and crude types who will have nothing to do with Christianity, abandoning it for a selfish life of pleasure, are evil through and through despite the superficial sympathy a member of the audience might feel toward them. "Nothing gives me such relief," continues the Third Torturer, "As murder a cut-purse or hang a thief" (435). He is the executive tool of justice, to be sure; but he is Pilate's lackey, and justice, usually the revenge of the state, is here carried out by one man against another under the most individualist of circumstances.

The second dominant device is the element of supportive mythomorphication. Individualism, when established, is continually shown up as the tool of the devil, and so undercut; conversely but with similar insistence, the story of Jesus' betrayal and execution is repeated time upon time, its proselytizing factors milked to their essence, till the crucifixion has become common coin, a normal natural part of life. Constant repetition of information, till the specifics of that information suffuse conscious life and render the original source of that information obscure, is one of the major methods of integration propaganda. Its goal is to convince its audience of its own objectivity: "Everybody knows that such-and-such is so" is the target sentiment of all integration propaganda. Just as "objectivity" and "value-free" standards are two of integration propaganda's contemporary products, so the literal "truth" of Jesus' life, of the miracles surrounding it, and of his martyrdom, were the tried-for products of a similar process six hundred years ago. In for example *The Pilgrims*, the betrayal/crucifixion story is presented for what seems like the nth time since the beginning of the Jesus section of the Cycle. Luke and Cleophas, in some of the most regular stanzas of the plays, present an extra-long exposition of what has already often been told—though, perhaps, not often enough for the propagandized message to set in. This repetition could be accounted for differently, perhaps pragmatically: the producers of the several plays did not get together beforehand so that each could decide what part of the Jesus story each wished to present. Had the Cycle been presented once only, such an explanation might, with some stretching of credibility, suffice; as a description of an annual fault, it lacks value. In actuality, such repetition should not be seen as a casual fault but as a consciously determined needed strength. Constant reiteration of known content serves both to reinforce the believing, and to convince, or throw fear into, those not believing. Only to the post-Cartesian linear rationalist did the conscious attempt to create mythomorphic truth through ritualized repetition become anathema.

This must be stressed: repetition and reiteration, even in ritual form, should not be seen as bad craftsmanship. But used at the wrong time in history it may show up the playwright as a bad judge of audience needs. It has been, in the past, easy enough to say that a theater which does not show clear and consistent cause and effect (motivation) has no place on the modern stage; and therefore the Wakefield Cycle, with the exception of much of *The Second Shepherds' Play*, is bad theater. Translated historically, such a statement would mean merely that late nineteenth and twentieth century audiences had not been trained to appreciate theater that attempted to communicate with its audience through a presentational surface which was in part technically ritualized. To an audience of the early fifteenth century a healthy mixture of rough mimetic presentation and constructed ritual would have seemed not at all unnatural. For such an audience it would have been difficult to say whether the even speeches of Luke and Cleophas or the garbled interchange of the shepherds made better theater.

This judgment of dramatic quality is quite different from the time-bound comment of certain commentators, among whose analyses Donald Clive Stuart's words ring appropriately false: "Herein lies the weakness of medieval drama: the theme is too great, too mysterious."[23] Stuart simply forgot that plays are written for audiences, and in the idiom of a specific audience. Ritualized presentation—and the Cycle abounds with it—is an easy idiom for the mysteries of religion; most religious institutions—Christian, eastern, and most primitive or pagan cults—have utilized such ritual forms to convince their congregations and followers that their leaders and their priests were capable of bringing what was invisible and ineffable into the sight and hearing of believers. As the medieval Church relaxed its use of ritual, theater took it up. The Church was losing its languages of suppression—for example: the magic of Latin;[24] its reliance on mystical generalization—as it grew weaker in its role of an institution of oppression; less and less would it be able to intervene between its congregation and the god it had made out of the reported teaching of Jesus Christ. As church ritual decreased and sermonizing in the vernacular increased, the feudal hegemony sought new modes, among them dramatic presentation, which could serve as a partial substitute for the needed expression of human life's greatest patterns.

But the new theater, though utilizing ritual presentation, had brought with it its own needs. Vernacular speech, contemporary problems that catered to an audience's sense of itself as a group or as a class independent of the sponsors and the producers—these would in the end help undermine the communal religious demands of the vested clergy and aristocracy.

The effective aesthetic tension of these medieval dramas, then, could be said to be the greatness of the theme —Eleanor Prosser calls it a "magnificent effrontery"[25]— standing in opposition to the daily concerns, the class-determined concerns, of the audience. Sometimes these elements do not act in unity; sometimes they fuse. But the aesthetic tension, that distinction between the first and third levels of consciousness that Jesus demanded be overcome in *The Pilgrims*, itself stands in constant con-

flict with the second level, on which the possibility of
political action is repressed or avoided.

From this perspective it is possible to speak of the
value system of the plays in terms of the intentions of its
ideology. So in *The Ascension of the Lord*, when John
says, "My Lord Jesus will work his will, / Plead we
never against his skill"; and Simon answers, "Steadfastly
to trust is best, / Unbelief begets much ill" (506), the
perspective of the telling stands visible on the surface.
Each man, we are told by the play, must subjugate his
individual thinking to Jesus' (read: the Church's) will:
the Christian revolution has been fought and won fourteen hundred years ago by Jesus himself, and any subsequent deviation is counterrevolutionary. And again,
when in *The Judgement* the evil souls huddle together
out of fear of an afterlife in torment, the Angel stands
above with sword in hand and shouts at them, "Stand not
together, part in two! / Together be ye not in bliss"
(523). The evil souls will be judged apart, separate from
the comfort of each other. Separation and alienation are
the dreaded ends to which anyone holding individualist
values must come, and the punishment fits the crime.
Grumbling together, as the shepherds were still capable
of doing on earth, is no longer allowed in the afterlife.

Nor is pleasure possible: the Cycle ends with a series
of descriptions of the hedonistic life, the ultimate titillations—the pleasures of eating and drinking, various
forms of the pleasures of sexuality. In an equally absolute fashion they are undercut by being placed in the
mouth of the demon Tutivillus, the collector of scraps
of liturgical phrases skipped or distorted in the performance of the Christian services. Tutivillus elaborates the
forms of titillation only to describe, subsequently, the
fate that awaits those who have acted out their pleasures.
Again however, the pleasures, once cited, cannot be
eradicated from the mind of the audience, and placing
their description here, at the very end of the Cycle, suggests a compromise on the part of the authors and the
sponsors. Tutivillus and his demon friends are exempt

from the horrors of hell because they stand *above* evil. This is a third possibility never made explicit in the Cycle, though hinted at occasionally: certain characters are dramatically attractive *because of* actions condemned by the Church. The individualistic grumbling of the shepherds remains one of their attractive mimetic qualities. The slapstick scatological humor of the torturers is more important in the play than their having reviled the crucified Jesus; in the end, unpunished and unrepentant, they are the play's moral spokesmen. Tutivillus, together with his cohorts, prancing about in judgment much like the Church itself, are allowed the pleasure of at least describing the fleshly delights which must be avoided.

At such moments the plays work against their basic hegemonic intentions. But immediately after such a teasing instant the audience is again caught up as the drama undermines the moment suggestive of the new values. In later centuries the individualistic ethic replaces, in other dramatic forms, the political conservatism of the Cycle's sponsors. But at the moment of the Cycle this individualism remains latent. The structure of the plays propagates the established order.

"I will not lose what I have made," remarked God at the beginning of *The Annunciation.* Nor, if they could help it, would the clergy, nor those who stood beside and behind them.

Chapter Five

SAMUEL BECKETT AND DRAMATIC

POSSIBILITIES IN AN AGE OF

TECHNOLOGICAL RETENTION

No serious critique of Samuel Beckett's work can exist in a cultural and political void. Conversely, any socially bound though self-conscious critique will serve a function parallel, but not necessarily similar, to that of Beckett's work itself.

There are three modes of critique that can pertain to Beckett's work. The first is a search for meaning within the work; it is here that the largest part of Beckett criticism has manifested itself. The second is the recognition that no *contentual* meaning exists within his work, and that whatever dramatic (or narrative) force is present— and there is considerable—results from a series of cultural forms which can only be understood historically. This formal aspect is relatively little examined, and I shall return to it below: it turns on Beckett's use of intellectual metahistory. The third and, for the purposes of a study of theater and propaganda, the most important mode of critique is an analysis of the historical importance and place, both for the theater and for the political society, of Beckett's contribution in rendering conscious a mid-twentieth century social reality of massive proportions, a reality which itself is historically and materially determined and, critically, largely unexamined. The largest segment of this examination will therefore deal less with Beckett, more with the nature of dramatic art-

work in an age of technological retention; but it is necessary to begin with Beckett. Beckett's dramatic work
marks the last (perhaps the most highly structured)
gasp, or statement, of a rich and fabulous form the
modern history of which dates back to, approximately,
the mystery plays. That is, the predominant mode of
communication through which European (and American) theater has functioned from the time of the Wakefield Cycle has been drawn from anti-intellectual life, as
both depicted and viewed. Life activity presented on the
stage was to have been perceived "directly," without the
aid of audience intellect, stealing across the darkened
senses to the mind. The cliché has run: if you have to
think about what it means and how it works *while you're
watching*, it can't be a good play. Beckett has proven to
be the last important playwright for whom that cliché
is valid.

The Search for Meaning

To search for the meaning of a work or part of a work is
a time-honored philological activity. Its products are
often valuable foundations on which to build a larger
awareness of some part of the work's and the society's
universe. By a close analysis of the parts and of their
relation to some larger part, or to a graspable whole,
philology was able to interpret and to reify images or
passages or metaphors into containable comprehendable
situations and activities. But Beckett renders such hermetic sleuthing virtually impossible. Its impossibility
does not, however, discourage the enthusiastic commentator, and so most resulting interpretations reduce the
work of Beckett to statements of The Dilemma of the
Modern Man, or some equivalent generalization, usually
meaningless. For one example among hundreds, Alfonso
Sastre: "Beckett takes his point of departure from [the]
circus pair. He destroys their external differences. He

rubs out the huge eyebrows. Takes off the big nose.
Erases the bright colours. Washes off the make-up, so
that the true sunken eyes appear. He throws the pair into
the circus ring. They are flung down. They wait. They
get bored. They play. We laugh, but our laughter rings
hollow. What has happened? We have recognized ourselves."[1] If *Waiting for Godot* is some sort of metaphor
for Man's Dilemma, the reader is not helped to an understanding of the Dilemma's oppressive parts by being presented with another metaphor. He or she wants to know
why it is necessary to employ a metaphor, how both
Beckett's metaphor and the Dilemma work, where the
Dilemma came from.

The genius of Beckett's work, especially of his drama,
is his avoidance of cohesive narrative content. Instead he
fills his plays with carefully juxtaposed units of cultural
junk. A piece of Cartesian rationalism here, a chunk of
Heidegger over there, a dash of pragmatism sprinkled
lethally; reference to Jesus on the cross at the beginning,
man as a thinking reed in the middle, shifts in master/
slave relationships, images of ashcans and dungheaps,
objectification of man into recorded voice, a return to the
question of suicide at the end; psychology, parapsychol-
ogy, metapsychology—all donate scraps of their vocabu-
laries. But in the end Beckett's plays are empty plays.
The pieces of what look like a theatrical universe are
present but do not hold together. Only the form of the
play keeps them in one piece. It is only partly the fault
of the bewildered commentator, nurtured on artists who
saw as their task the establishment of unity out of a
fragmented society, that he or she turns away from the
work and into the self for a cohesive form to hold Beckett's mess, a gestalt to control the chaos. The work, the
play, became in the fifties and the sixties a dramatic
Rorschach test for the commentator, and explication became a statement of one's own (shallow or perhaps profound) unexplored perception of The Dilemma, saving
from Beckett's work those scraps supportive of the critical

presentation, repressing those fragments, equally present, which were irrelevant to the commentary. The priest sees Beckett as Christian, the psychoanalyst understands *Godot* as a statement of schizophrenia, the social scientist speaks perhaps of alienation. Each person interprets and codifies some few bits and pieces of the work according to his or her own specialization.

All these attitudes try to take Beckett's details seriously. The problem with such literalness is this: Beckett only describes; he does not celebrate the phenomena he describes. An audience's pleasure in his work grows from the stark accuracy of his idiom and in the sharp edges of his descriptions; the specific meanings imposed on Beckett's work result from the order in which he himself has presented the chaos around him to his audiences, according to his celebrated maxim, "To find a form that accommodates the mess, that is the task of the artist now."[2] The danger with which any reader or viewer of Beckett must always be prepared to deal is the assumption that Beckett is personally supportive of the fragments of value and philosophy stated by his fictions and his dramas. Beckett's is an empty theater, wherein each viewer sees reflected only the fragments, the semirelated details with which one would normally, in one's own daily experience of existence, attempt to cope. On this first level, then, Beckett is the purely neutral writer, merely establishing, describing, noting. In terms of his plays' contents, his commentators have rarely allowed him his role.

The Search for Form

There can be no denying that Beckett's work contains a series of recurring cross-references. Bicycles, atomizers, walking sticks, shoes, many *things*: these cross-references have a relationship, and the relationship has a form because the cross-references are juxtaposed to make a form that accommodates the fragments. The basic form is the failed quest, in five parts (on which I shall elaborate, below) : Movement I; Impasse I; Movement II; Impasse II; Deterioration.[3] The second Movement is weaker than the first, and in the second Impasse the mover collaborates with the obstruction. The pattern functions on a series of levels. It exists within the scenes of the plays to create the building blocks that comprise the whole play. Most often several series of the pattern exist simultaneously, one event serving as, let us say, the first Impasse to one series and as the second to another—or the entirety of a series might function as, say, the second Impasse to a larger sequence. Further, the pattern structures the entirety of each play—and, it should be noted, of each novel as well.[4]

Though the failed quest is, potentially, a partial element in an organic life cycle (human or social), there is nothing within such a cycle to suggest that this particular form is necessary and natural to man's life or to the life of his institutions at all times. Nonetheless, Beckett's action of utilizing this form to accommodate his universe should not be considered a merely artificial and therefore useless activity. Imposed form is the first step, within the best tradition of avoiding the chaos of a fragmented universe, in the attempt to understand the otherwise ungraspable relations between apparently irreconcilable phenomena, between *things* in general:[5] man as hypothesis builder.

For Beckett's work such a critique can take place only subsequent to the initial observation that all the material in the plays is a clutter of meaningless cultural junk: each play is filled with events, facts, references without narrational (that is, contentual) meaning for the play. But beyond this first level of chaos one is left with the nagging sense that perhaps all these fragmented events and circumstances do serve a function after all; and then meaning begins only if the bits and fragments are presented in an ordered juxtaposition. The only meaning in the play is the sequence of things, of events, of episodes.

Such a sequence establishes the pattern of the search that deteriorates into failure.[6] Any specific event or circumstance or thing or phenomenon could be replaced by any other with virtually no loss of meaning, just so long as the form of each event, the five-step process toward deterioration, remained consistent with the overall structure.

Perhaps the best demonstration of this process would be a series of explications from *Endgame* which could illustrate several of the functions the process may serve. The whole pattern is easiest to see when writ small. I take, then, as a first example a point about two-thirds of the way through the play (E57):[7]

Movement I: Clov begins to pick up objects lying on the ground.

Impasse I: Hamm interrupts him by demanding an explanation.

Movement II: Clov gives the explanation and goes back to work.

Impasse II: A variation on the question and explanation leads to Hamm's exasperation and Clov's continual but weakened coping, "I'm doing my best to create a little order," concluding in Hamm's imposed command, "Drop it!"

Deterioration: The process and the incident end when Clov goes toward the door, giving up.

This scene, together with dozens similar to it, serves as one of the smallest building blocks in the structure of the play. Each such episode functions as paradigm to the whole.

The process need not be integrated into dialogue. Equally as easily it can take place in a soliloquy. In the prelude to Clov's final long speech, for example (E80–81):

Movement I: Clov talks to himself about those who once talked to him about gaining perspective through love, through friendship, through dying.

Impasse I: Hamm attempts to stop Clov's chatter.

Movement II: Clov ignores Hamm, and continues by

commenting on the kind of despair that leads to nothing but a totally blank future for himself.

Impasse II: A retrospective glance at the past is so filled with unrelated detail as to give him no perspective whatsoever: "I am so bowed I only see my feet, . . . I say to myself that the earth is extinguished, though I never saw it lit."

Deterioration: The declaration of an end is purely formal, and without connection to his previous soliloquy: "This is what we call making an exit." The poverty of movement, when present, reduces surface tension to a minimum; what remains is the dramatic conflict.

Or to take a longer sequence, the incident with the telescope (E28–30):

Movement I: Clov goes for the glass, returns with it, leaves again for the ladder, climbs up.

Impasse I: Clov discovers he does not have the glass; he cannot look out of the window.

Movement II: Clov goes off, finds the glass, returns. He climbs up the ladder, looks through it at the audience, reports, "I see . . . a multitude . . . in transports . . . of joy." Then he looks outside the window.

Impasse II: He sees nothing: "Zero, zero and zero."

Deterioration: "All is what?" asks Hamm. "Corpsed," says Clov. He looks out again and says finally, "The light has sunk." And with these words begins another discussion, astronomical and geological in nature, which is itself describable in terms of the sequential paradigm.

Not all building block sequences are so easily discernible. Pieces of a sequence, for example, may be imbedded into the play at nonconsecutive points. These pieces are then secondary, and merely supportive to the primary structuring elements. A good example in *Endgame* is the series of incidents surrounding the toy dog, the animal mentioned very briefly very early in the play (E 2) and introduced finally about halfway through.

Movement I (E 39–41): Clov brings Hamm a black toy dog with three legs; they discuss its color, its sex, its missing ribbon, its inability to stand. The dog falls down.

Impasse I (E 56–57): Hamm reaches for the dog and cannot find it; Clov gives it to him, noting it is not a real dog; Hamm throws it away.
Movement II (E 67–68): Hamm asks for the dog, but doesn't really want it; his request is far weaker than before, paralleling his general condition at this point in the play.
Impasse II (E 76–77): Clov uses the dog as a club and hits Hamm over the head with it. The dog falls to the ground. Hamm asks for it again, Clov gives it to him with the admonition, "Hit me with the gaff. Not with the dog." Even as a club the dog is useless. Hamm "takes it in his arms."
Deterioration (E 84): As his final gesture in the play, Hamm discards the dog, then unfolds his handkerchief and covers his face with it. The moment of throwing the dog down also serves as the second Impasse in another sequence, Hamm's final speech.

The largest example of the sequence toward deterioration is of course the structure of the play altogether. The Hamm/Clov elements form the central element of structure, interrupted and so reinforced—interruption as integral to the deterioration process—by the Nell/Nagg elements. Each of the larger segments may serve a single or a double function: so the first Movement in the Nell/Nagg (N/N) series becomes the first Impasse in the Hamm/Clove (H/C) series. Or the series may overlap: Hamm silences Nagg (E 23) and so breaks off the Impasse in the H/C series while creating an Impasse in the N/N series; the process toward Impasse II in the H/C series (E 23–56) also contains the second, weaker Movement in the N/N series (E 49–56). In addition, each of the larger segments, the Movements or the Impasses, is still comprised of the small units (juxtaposed and/or disperse building block sequences) which give the play its texture and which condition the audience's mind to accepting the pattern of the overall structure.

An outline of the overall structure of *Endgame* would be valuable at this point:

HAMM/CLOV SERIES

(E 1–14) *Movement I*: Hamm and Clov talk; Nagg appears and slows down their discussion.

(E 14–23) *Impasse I*: No Hamm or Clov.

(E 23–36) *Movement II*: Hamm silences Nagg, goes on to a dominant active role that begins to dissipate (E 36–56).

(E 56–82) *Impasse II*: Begins with the impossible attempt to clear away objects generally (E 57, discussed above), ends with the departure of Clov.

(E 82–84) *Deterioration*: The end of Hamm, the end of the series, the end of the play.

NELL/NAGG SERIES

(E 14–23) *Movement I*: Nagg takes over the whole of the play in discussion with Nell.

(E 23–49) *Impasse I*: Nell and Nagg are out of the picture.

(E 49–55) *Movement II*: Nagg without Nell, searching for pleasures, willing even to pray to God.

(E 56) *Impasse II*: Now there are no more sugar plums: all the pleasures have disappeared.

(E 56) *Deterioration*: Nagg sinks into his bin and himself disappears after calling Nell; silence from him for the rest of the play.

The two largest series interact; similarly they are comprised of segments themselves interacting with other (previous, subsequent, and simultaneous) segments. The final speech of the play, Hamm's long swan song, which begins with Clov's exit, contains the final element in the toy dog sequence, serves as the deterioration segment for the Hamm/Clov series, and is itself a full series, the play writ small in one speech. So Hamm, in the last moment before the very last, decides to play: "Me to play." (Pause. Wearily.) "Old endgame lost of old, play and lose and have done with losing" (E 82). He then plays by discussing with himself what he shall discard—the gaff, the toy dog—and backs off when he cannot see out of his glasses (Impasse I). He overcomes the impasse physically by wiping off his glasses and intellectually by phrasing well the nature of his circumstances; when he can congratulate himself ("Nicely put, that"—E 83), he can also move on to his last empty philosophication. The specfic words of this are interchangeable with any other words; the discussion of whether he should be with his father (or whomever) and his father with him is interchangeable with any other discussion, so long as the emphasis is on impotent (physical or speculative) movement. He calls to his father, there is no response, the last and tiniest of possibilities has not been achieved, the last Impasse has not been overcome; at this point he finally throws away the toy dog. He acquiesces at last to his circumstance, unfolds the handkerchief, covers his face with it. "You . . . remain" are the last words (E 84), and the play ends with a long stage silence.

Multiple simultaneity is the essence of tight theater. The larger the number of controlled interactive elements —language, action, color, exposition, movement, plot, whatever—the more complex the play will be. (Such complexity can of course be played against apparently simple moments to great effect.) The simultaneity of multiple deterioration sequences gives Beckett's plays their power and their horror: the critical common denominator even in the most disperse analyses of Beckett's works is usually the easy "nothing and all" simultaneity, the supermetaphysical approach of existential wailing that "All is nothing" or some equivalent juxtaposition of the two concepts.[8] The specific elaborations of the all/ nothing simultaneity harken back to the critical Rorschach test syndrome, a phenomenon which itself can be reduced to the language of the syndrome: there is nothing in Beckett's work except form, therefore any interpretation is available to one seeking out his own meaning of the content. This blatant contradiction is itself culturally bound; the third section of this chapter will examine the kinds of perspective necessary to analyze both the bind and the culture, and to begin to overcome the propaganda that reinforces both.

The final effect of a Beckett play is to disallow the perspective necessary to critique it. Almost everyone, for example, has noted that the two parts of *Godot* are supposed to be two days. But the issue is not whether or not the days are tangential, or which comes first. Rather, the central effect of the two days, the two acts, is that they present only one perspective: that any given day or brief series of days provides one with no external perspective whatsoever as to the implications of the larger human questions. What is man, and what is his function, are questions not merely not answered by the play, they are questions not asked by the written play. Certainly the play provokes these questions in the minds of members of the audience—but such provocation is the beginning of critical interpretation, the beginning of individuation and fragmentation by the audience. This audience has been trained by its society to interpret and thereby explain human difficulties (not human impossibilities, however) by casting their difficulties into the confines of highly institutionalized thought processes.

While audience avoidance of contextual and cultural critique is the usual subsequence of a Beckett play, that is not necessarily the goal of the play. The plays implicitly tell the audience: all days are all the same, all people are all the same; habit is the deadener, and time brings about deterioration. Beckett's plays neither celebrate nor negate such habit. Beckett's talent is his ability to walk *the very narrow line between the celebration and the negation of thoughtless daily activity*. Habits, disconnected social and political and religious and philosophical and pragmatic habits: these are the bits of cultural junk that make up his plays and explain why any scrap can replace any other scrap: because habit is impotence. As early as the writing of *Proust* Beckett was well aware of the possibilities as well as of the dangers of habit:

> At this point, and with a heavy heart and for the satisfaction or disgruntlement of Gideans, semi and integral, I am inspired to concede a brief parenthesis to all

the analogivorous, who are capable of interpreting the
"Live dangerously," that victorious hiccough in vacuo,
as the national anthem of the true ego exiled in habit.
The Gideans . . . imply a hierarchy of habits, as
though it were valid to speak of good habits and bad
habits. An automatic adjustment of the human organ-
ism to the conditions of its existence has as little moral
significance as the casting of a clout when May is in or
out; and the exhortation to cultivate a habit as little
sense as an exhortation to cultivate a coryza. (Pp. 8–9)

The plays always hint at the possibility of overcoming
habit; victory, or optimism, or possibility is the suggested
thrust of the Movement episodes of the plays. But ultimately habit deadens all entirely.

The line between a negation and a celebration of habit
is so narrow as to be almost invisible. Further, such a line
itself is merely a hypothetical separation, formed by the
possibility of celebration of habit on one side, the possibility of negation on the other. The line is established
only by the material on either side of it. In this manner,
the line between the possibilities was rarely recognized
in the fifties; it was usually merely felt. Dramatic and
social analysis could not hold onto an (as yet) unstated
hypothesis, and few had the historical perspective to
render it visible with a critique of the contradiction between celebration and negation—with a critique of the
material Beckett had presented. For an audience sufficiently distanced from its past, Beckett seemed to bemoan
the point to which that past had brought his characters
(and so, the western world); for an audience beyond that
past, a progressive or radical audience, let us say, he
seemed to be celebrating a destructive contemporary
circumstance.

But the line between celebration and negation is time-
bound, and time provides the perspective which later
renders visible and significant a moment from the past.
Beckett too was aware of the possibility of increased visibility through a shift in temporal perspective, though he

presented the possibility primarily on the level of individual perception:

> . . . if, *by accident*, and given favourable circumstances (a relaxation of the subject's habit of thought and a reduction of the radius of his memory, a general diminished tension of consciousness following upon a phase of extreme discouragement), if by some miracle of analogy the central impression of a past sensation recurs as an immediate stimulus which can be instinctively identified by the subject with the model of duplication . . . , then the total past sensation, not its echo nor its copy, but the sensation itself, annihilating every spatial and temporal restriction, comes in a rush to engulf the subject in all the beauty of its infallible proportion. (P. 54)

Beckett was, at this early point in his career, still caught within rationalism. He was aware of the processes necessary to transcend it, but had not yet done so. Later, in the plays, he depicts characters who have not transcended the blindness of the immediate historical moment either. If Beckett's intention was to depict this lack of perspective so that a play may in fact provide "some miracle of analogy," then the play succeeds as stimulant to awareness only insofar as the audience can use the play for such progressive ends as subsume and solve the huge paradoxes presented by the play itself. But when individual members of the audience each fragment the play to suit individual needs, when interpretation returns a member of the audience to deadening comforting habit, then the play has not merely failed, it has been conscripted by the forces of habit back into the ideology of the institutionalized culture.

From this perspective, Beckett's work in describing habit has contributed, for most members of the audience, to the deadening of sensibilities, as in Estragon's infamous opening words in *Godot*, "Nothing to be done," or Hamm's "It's the end of the day like any other day, isn't it, Clov?" (E 13). Except to a critical consciousness that

stands entirely outside of and so apart from the play,
Beckett's plays do not function as the negation to episodes (dramatic or daily), such as those he is describing.
Though it would be too much to say he celebrates his
vision of the world, nonetheless his work serves as the
final voice of support for the old historical habit of fragmenting individualism. Twenty years after *Godot*, a
retrospective view of the narrow line which the plays of
Beckett ran and a retrospective comprehension of the
bourgeois intellectuality of the fifties into which they
were born, taken together, point to the proper relationship between Beckett's work and his audiences and explain the Rorschach critical success of his plays. The
implication will therefore be strong that the usual simultaneity of values and systems between a play and its
audience, the simultaneity which lets the audience call
the play "good," was in Beckett's case doubly reinforced:
his absence of content was for a fifties audience itself
both a recognizable statement and the abstraction to
which each member of the audience could hitch his lack
of perspective. As a bonus, there was no story to get in
the way.

Dramatic Art in an Age of Technological Retention

But this is not to be a cultural analysis of the fifties;
rather, on the level at which Beckett's plays are indeed
part of the last gasp of a fabulous form of theater, the
necessary procedure lies in comprehending the audience
that found (or still finds) the work of Beckett speaking
directly to its needs: Why did (or do) members of Beckett's audiences allow the plays to be imposed upon their
minds as tests which explicate audience mentality rather
than the purpose of the plays, and so become perfect ex-
emplars of integration propaganda? (To some extent, of
course, all art is enjoyed more when the details presented
can be personalized; but there is most often a return to
the artwork.) Clearly, Beckett was telling his audiences

something they could not hear from anyone else. Though many other writers had spoken (at length) of the Dilemma of Modern Man, or of similar anesthetizing and obscuring euphemisms (like "absurd"), there was a difference: Beckett was addressing himself to change. He took his material from the force and the might of four hundred years of individualist genius, creation, and proud predominance, and depicted its deterioration toward *impotence*. (Beckett in *Three Dialogues*: "I'm working with impotence, ignorance. I don't think impotence has been exploited in the past.") Hence, the constructive power of his *techniques* was not visible. The techniques were felt, merely. But ultimately they would contribute in a positive fashion to the audience's (unverbalized) desire for possible change. That change could be evolutionary or revolutionary, violent or smooth, it did not matter which. (And these distinctions within the concept of change were the barest of concepts —and still far from issues—in the early fifties.)

The kinds of basic changes that have taken place since the appearance of *Waiting for Godot* suggest some of the possibilities for change which were the least of seedlings to the consciousness of the fifties, revolutions of differing sorts, some of which have, by the early seventies, reached a level of material reality. A tangential exploration of these seeds now becomes important in order to place Beckett's plays back within the context of his audience.

The most obvious change in the west in the last twenty years has been a cultural revolution of massive proportions. This cultural revolution at first asked and then exhorted the individual to explore the vast possibilities of personal life-style, and of existence altogether. Taken alone, within a margin at bottom ideologically individualist, such a revolution, even if totally successful, is no more than a set of private pleasures, most often elitist in nature, which lend their practitioner a (false) sense of freedom within a society that holds him, economically and socially, a propagandized prisoner of forces he does not understand. Sexy anticonservative clothes, orgasmic dancing, inhibitional release through drugs—life can be fun, but most often in a late bourgeois technology this fun screens the social control devices of the hegemony which must supply an escape valve to its society in order to remain in control. The cultural revolution can under these circumstances be seen as a titillating bedazzlement of the individual that keeps him from more serious activities, such as his participation in a political revolution. But a cultural revolution can backfire, and to some extent this one did. It provided a platform, built out of individual and daily human experience, from which a larger and suddenly an economic and political perspective was possible. Once the technology of sound amplification, the chemistry of the drug trip, and the shortness of the skirt could not be taken further *within* the established, the political, culture (i.e., within an abbreviated revolution), it became necessary to expand the platforms of change beyond the merely cultural level. It became essential to establish a larger foundation for further, and different, revolution. This process, reaching its first big plateau in the late sixties, could be called a communicational revolution.[9]

To some extent the (early) desire of the communicational revolution was to disseminate the cultural revolution to a popular audience, a process which would change the nature of the cultural revolution from elitist to popular. (For the cultural revolution entrepreneur, the possibility of new markets in a still highly capitalist technology was of course a considerable stimulant in the dissemination; the hegemony's technology controlled and controls the media of mass dissemination.) But large-scale communication activities do not merely sell ever more products. Except in the most tightly censored society—which late capitalism cannot be; it must have its freedoms to increase its markets—communications media sell products and *simultaneously* metasell the sense of possible change. Individual possibility is the paramount by-product, but social possibility is also available. And once the potential of basic social change has been implanted in a society's consciousness, there is (virtually) no getting it out. Ultimately the sequence will be complete: from cultural revolution to communicational revolution to political revolution. The first two of these revolutionary processes are usually lacking in a new ideology; the unrefined human desire for freedom leaves them chaotic and disperse. (Beckett: "To find a form that accommodates the mess, that is the task of the artist now.") Political revolution demands an ideological paradigm to shape those implicit human freedoms merely felt by its precursors. Political revolution positions an individualistically oriented cultural revolution at a point within the processes of change where that cultural revolution can become integral to human/social improvement. Political revolution helps the communicational revolution evolve itself from a medium for the dissemination of elitist materials to a series of activist organs, organs which render their users (if these users desire to remain consistent with the impulses toward freedom and survival which activated the original cultural revolution) part of an organization for political revolution.

A simultaneity rather than a sequentiality of these separate revolutionary processes would in its own way be a great work of art; but such an occurrence is for the moment unlikely. Previously, revolution has existed, and so continues to be thought of, as a national phenomenon. The time of national revolution is coming to a close. In the industrial society the time may already have passed by. Any western revolution will be internationally intellectual, technologically controlled, mass-based, and transnationally economic in effect.

Which takes us back to literature, and to Beckett. To a considerable extent the cultural revolution was an individualistic reaction against modernism (in both literature and life-style), the cultural revolution-as-individualism showing itself off in society at large (in life-style, dress, dance, and the like), in opposition to modernism-as-individualism cloistered hermetically in the mind.

Beckett, *in terms of the content of his work* (structure, material, style), is the last of the modernists. In Beckett's work, a kind of menopause of modernism cohabits with a series of techniques that depict change as the basic order of existence. Further, the techniques make it clear that for Beckett simultaneity through multilayered exhibition (dramatic presentation) leads to that change.

In this respect, Beckett's work is the precursor of an art form that will look very different from Beckett's own when it is one day achieved. His work portrays, in microcosm, a system of available materials, a system which is already revolutionizing the nature of processes of human change: ever increasingly the stimulants to and artifacts of change are capable of being retained technologically. That is, they are no longer lost to history. Retention of the work of art is becoming the major element in the change of human awareness. For example: visual portrayal of times past—the popular film, or the news action as recorded on videotape—by virtue of retaining not merely activity but the implicit ideology within which that activity is based, depicts in the most convincing fashion the shift in values by placing the artwork in the setting of the contemporary audience. "It's dated" becomes a statement of ideological fact that recognizes a shift in value systems. Not merely dress, but also attitudes to and perception of daily reality, date with time.

This, as conscious humans, we have always known; but till the twentieth century we have never had the ability to measure our synchronically limited experience against a past that was more than the vaguest of (personal or interpreted historical) memories. To the extent that the institutions of awareness—scholarship, for example—have attempted to provide and retain the sense of an evolutionary history within which to place artifacts of and stimulants to change, the hegemonic institutions of each age required their integration propagandists to destroy the sense, indeed the very possibility, of historical change. But today, the retention, classification, and historical continuity of artifacts that may be dealt with by popular audiences can, for the first time ever, provide twenty-first century persons with a sense of history. A source of the sense of history was of course potentially available through retained artifacts during certain moments in human history—most recently through books and libraries. But books and literacy have been the property of the privileged few, and have by and large been used for purposes of domination. Literacy itself, as we have seen, has been used by integration propaganda as a façade of freedom, and so as an instrument of control. But technological retention renders an awareness of historical change a potentially common popular experience.

To the credit of modernism, retention was a major element in its aesthetics: time and myths and objects and traditions were soldered on to its corpus, and caressed lovingly. In terms of its content, the work of Beckett is in this tradition, that of the great individualist experiments to transcend the binds of their rational linear (and capitalist and bourgeois) forms—Joyce and Proust and Faulkner and Woolf, Dadaism and surrealism and futurism. But the limitations of the modernists were also built into their aesthetics: each in his art attempted to utilize the greatest achievements of individualistic method. Proust's *cogito* is only the most blatant example. Joyce's *Finnegans Wake* takes the experiment of retention through the individual mind to its extreme. In this sense, someone like Robbe-Grillet capsulizes in the microcosm of his work the processes of modernism from Proust to the end of Joyce: *The Erasers* is to Swann as the virtually invisible narrator of *La Maison de rendez-vous* is to the multilingual puppet strings pulled by Joyce over the wake. I mention Robbe-Grillet here only to suggest that, even in a generation following Beckett's, experiments in the individualistic exploration of the mind continue: *Maison de rendez-vous* is almost completely (two tiny exceptions) *un roman sur rien*, achieving Flaubert's pure form, if by *rien* we mean external society and by form we mean the absolute mind. For, by the time of *Finnegans Wake* and/or *La Maison de rendez-vous*, nothing is left of that outside world which the history of the novel, traditionally, had attempted to comprehend and explain. Where to go then, in fictive creation (whether dramatic or narrative), if realism of the old descriptive sort feels outworn, and the explorations of mind circumcursed by modernists of whatever generation no longer seem possible? Where to go in dramatic production if one agrees, as one must, with Darko Suvin when he notes, "After *Waiting for Godot*, writing dramas like Eliot or Williams, Camus or later Ionesco is no doubt still factually possible, but it can no longer be regarded as a significant artistic pursuit"?[10] The twofold answer to the double question is complex. Partly the question itself is misleading; it has usually been phrased in terms which implicitly accept the moral superiority of privilege, hence it has hidden a series of possible answers.

It is, however, possible to disseminate forms once controlled by the privileged few to larger audiences. For a long time the concept of theater in the provinces, for example, was looked down upon as a theater for those who could not make it in the city (whichever city), as second- or third-rate. Among the producers of great theater in western Europe and in the Americas, only in Germany was there a serious noncentralized theater.[11] Broader presentation of standard dramatic materials is certainly possible, or the same known material can be used by new playwrights for other ends—the musical as a form of social critique for example, learning from the lesson taught by television advertising that people will listen to anything so long as it is well sung; and the cabaret has always used music for satiric ends.

Instead of broader presentation of materials, some theater of the sixties utilized another elitist form, generally found under the rubric of radical theater. Some of this functioned as agitation propaganda. More often, because it could be so easily dismissed, it served the purposes of the integration propagandist. By and large so-called radical theater was an arbitrary collective of theater folk, feigning communality, who cursed their

audiences for being insufficiently radical. At its best, this
kind of theater contributed to the cultural revolution.
Political change was many movements away.
These first parts of the answer have been tried. They
are unsatisfactory, in any kind of large way, as adequate
media of presentation, to such an audience as had felt the
need to interpret itself through Beckett's plays. In these
plays Beckett's audiences saw reflected, whether correctly
or not, the material basis of their lives. It is this basis to
which a theater in search of serious popular success will
ultimately address itself. The second large element of the
answer posed by Suvin's comment has been, till now, virtually unelaborated. This element will be an art form
that is both narrative and nonlinear, both individual and
collective—a theater that avoids simple naturalism and
unheightened daily experience in order to present social
and individual reality on its stages.
   This form of theater will certainly take into cogni-
zance the essential need for social description in a popular idiom—along the lines of a Dickens novel in the nineteenth century, let us say, or in the twentieth even a
sports event or a television soap opera (in the sense of
either "All in the Family" or the "Secret Storm" or the
"Forsyte Saga"). Further, it will utilize the psychic
experiments of hermetic modernism for its own ends. A
member of the popular audience would no longer be able
to say of, for example, a piece of fiction, "It's a great
novel but I couldn't get through it"—a statement heard
either when the work is clever, ingrown, terribly complicated, scholarly, subtle, or intricate, and evermore increasingly when the work is written down (much easier
to go to a movie or to watch television).
   Here then is the beginning of the crux: not only is
popular idiom essential, so also is popular form. In the
eighteenth century, fiction became more popularly satisfying than poetry or theater because it was accessible to a
much larger group. In the first half of the twentieth century film took predominance over reading; in the second
half television has taken predominance over film. The

reason is the same: each new medium rendered its material more accessible to a popular audience[12] than could its predecessor. The difficulty in accepting, in the first half of the century, film as art (a battle since won; but is television an art form? the battle has barely begun to rage) suggests a transformation, in Walter Benjamin's terms, not in kinds of art, but of "the entire nature of art."[13] What in fact determines the nature and limit of artistic possibility other than the technology available to and inventable by the maker? And there is no need to limit the question of artistic possibility to the acceptance of television as an art form. A basic intention of the artistic process is to produce the artifact in order to retain its meaning (as with the modernists: myths, memories, past times, etc.; or with the capitalists: technological retention and reproduction for capital gain). In a similar sense there is every reason to believe that in, for example, some science-fiction future, technological retention will come to mean the ability to tap one's own brain in order to re-create past experience within past value-structures: from the chaos of contemporary hallucinatory and psychedelic experience derived from arbitrarily taken and arbitrarily activating drugs, to the total control of chemistry and electronic stimulation (from the confusion of the Wright brothers to the Boeing 747—itself still a chaos compared to the space or magnetic tunnel travel of the future). Similarly, the artist's ability may, at some time in the future, come to be measured in terms of his ability to create a machine that touches an electrode to the lobes of the brain to tap long-lost memories which are then translated into electronic waves which are recombined easily on any home television screen. Improbable perhaps, but so was film, and so was printing.

Beckett has not transformed art but he has, by using art to depict impotence (the last unexploited individualist sphere), demonstrated with frightening implicitness that the late twentieth century concept of art is in profound need of transformation. His techniques show the way, though his content is borrowed from his predecessors. The voices of his characters are fully idiomatic though ever increasingly, in both the plays and the novels, he has worked his style toward hermetic modernism, long since tried. Indeed, if impotence and silence are his goal, then he has need of no better model than modernism itself.

Beyond Beckett, popular idiom and an as yet untried, unlabeled postmodernism will combine to create a third mode of expression, one which utilizes electronic media in an attempt at popular communication. By popular communication I do not mean mass communication. Mass communication occurs when one turns on a television set in the 1970's. Mass communication is an elitist controlled and so repressive form. Rather, by popular I mean the many working classes as a series of communities of discrete workers, conscious of themselves as individuals and as members of a community, workers who are, in both circumstances, not the dead ends of a communications process. Rather these workers would be participants who return new information, a new set of stimuli, to the electronic source and so render the communications program an interactive and so open system. Beckett's audiences engaged in Rorschach activities because this was the only outlet for their stimulated and immediately stifled imaginations, the only outlet advised or allowed by the integration propaganda they had been fed. They were entirely caught within a closed system.

Given the circumstance of a responding technological audience, the very media of communication would be transformed from their present state, which has demanded a passive audience, to a point at which these media would come to *require* active audience involvement, both simultaneous with the moment of production and in the future. Brecht among others had spoken of active audience involvement with radio many years earlier.[14] Among the possible results: direct rather than representative participation in government; no more elections and repressive legislatures; government by information, by need and response.

Most importantly, the extent to which art, for present purposes dramatic art, manages to succeed by bringing about changed circumstances in a society cannot be measured in terms of any immediately causal actions. Rather, the best of art-as-agitation results in so valid a description of reality as to render it immediately recognizable to each member of the audience, so that he and she are brought to the necessary moment of awareness which *at some future time* will allow them to be triggered into action.[15] This may demand many art-experiences, experiences of reality through an art phenomenon as mediator, before the members of the audience will participate in a revolutionary act. The only direct changes brought about by a revolutionary artwork are psychic-intellectual; such changes can ultimately *lead* to a supersaturation of the mind with a clearer consciousness of reality, a supersaturation which can be crystallized into action when the member of society sees a forced and inorganic process being imposed on some segment of that society. That is to say, it is naïve to assume that the work of art will ever lead large groups of people, in any cause-and-immediate-effect way, to man the barricades; *the work of art is not real—it is an artifact*, and no matter how completely convincing the artwork may be, it has a limited space and a specific duration which separate it off into its own closed system from the rest of society.

It is no wonder, then, that the work of art does not cause large numbers of people to react immediately to barbarisms and other social horrors depicted by the work of art—one cannot, in a society built of learned disconnections, get too excited over something which is, in the end (its own), artificial. As a form of goading into action, the work of art is bound to fail; but goading was never its function. The work of art is, at best, reality once removed. The best of nineteenth century realism is once removed from social reality; the best of modernism is once removed from psychic (often literary and/or intellectual) reality. It is difficult enough for firsthand, that is, experienced, reality to move people to action; how much more difficult, if not impossible, for written or painted or acted or danced reality, with its merely vicarious relation to its models, to function as the ultimate motivating force. It is not the failure of the artwork to move societies to change which must be decried; rather we must condemn the failure of most analyses, as opposed to the dialectic critique, of art to understand the function and place of art in any historical and so perhaps ultimately revolutionary process.

In the end only an understanding of the direct connection between material social circumstances and material social oppression will bring about change. Art can act, at best, as the indicator that makes oppression recognizable as a condition socially/temporally imposed, that makes acceptance of oppression visible as a product of integration propaganda. Artworks can keep an oppressive condition from remaining accepted and acceptable as the natural state of the oppressed population. Time-bound art is often successful because it speaks to, attacks, agitates against specific (hence momentary) negative social circumstances which stand between immediate social reality and potentially recognizable historical reality. Retention, classification, and subsequent popular availability of the artifact can provide the basis for that source of history which allows the artifact its place in the dialectical process.

The place of art, then, within the premise of dialectical materialism that "it is not men's consciousness that determines their existence, but on the contrary their social existence which determines their consciousness," begins to come clear. Social existence determines, in Raymond Williams' and Gramsci's sense that it limits the various possibilities for, consciousness. Such marginal forms of social consciousness create both the artwork and the technology which surrounds the artwork. The feudal or bourgeois artwork is the product of a limited, hence determined, society. Technology, by placing any artwork within a popularly recognizable, popularly communicable series of media, can begin to undermine the intentions of those who are in control of both the economic institutions and the institutions of consciousness—who are in control of the form given to social existence. If that existence is within repressive circumstances, then a valid (antirepressive, nonrepressive, postrepressive) artwork will be the expression of human possibilities more natural than the experiences provided by daily social existence. The experience of the few, or even of a single artist, made into a work of art, can be a more inherently valid response to human need than the institutionalized experience called social existence, which a repressive society through its propagandized comforts imposes on itself. The artwork, created by a consciousness within (though perhaps at the fringes of) social existence, transcends social existence and attains a formal relationship (critique, imposition) to social existence delivered from *outside* (spatially beyond, temporally ahead of) that daily social existence. That work of art is most valid which is most quickly recognizable by the many as a more valid formulation of human needs (and responses to those needs).[16]

But the artwork does not affect widespread consciousness until the technology, formally part and parcel of social existence, provides media for the popular dissemination of the artwork. Social existence determines technology; technology normally reinforces social existence; but technology and its communications media are also capable of changing consciousness. They do so when the work of art (that more valid expression of human possibilities, either as critique of social existence or as a model for a less contradictory existence) becomes the content for dissemination. Print, that technological product of late-medieval social existence, changed the very structure of human consciousness, even though Gutenberg's (and others') intentions may well have been far more conservative. Similarly, radio and more recently television, tools mainly in the hands of the repressive technology, have already changed (though not yet revolutionized) social existence even with a *minimum* of content that could be deemed artistically valid. The possibilities ahead are enormous.

The artwork disseminated through popularly controlled technology represents the greatest potential for breaking down a propagandized and apparently closed system of social existence. As a collectivity of a series of ideologically similar artifacts, the technologically popularized and communicated artform can bring about a change of consciousness in the larger audience—that is, in the society. The change of consciousness grows out of a change in social existence and results in a new series of descriptions of the nature of social existence, in new paradigms. The change as realized follows thereafter, either through external violence or through the internal attempt to pre-empt large-scale change by allowing visible change. As the contradictions come closer to the surface the revolutionary process picks up speed. Revolutionary art, properly disseminated, acts as mediator between, on the one hand, individual and collective human consciousness, and on the other, the potential change in the material basis of daily existence.

If this critique seems to have ranged far from Beckett's plays, let me insist that the preceding is necessary for an understanding of how these plays related, and relate, to their audiences. In addition, the contextual discussion is a great deal closer to the plays and to the climate— theatrical and social—they themselves have helped create than may appear obvious at first glance. Beckett's plays, after their introduction to, though hardly their assimilation in, elitist consciousness on a large scale (that is, after the "popularity" of *Godot*), ceased to function as pieces of cultural revolution; instead they became part of the communicational revolution. The plays broke dramatic structure down into its component parts—the tradition of dramatic structure itself being a piece of cultural junk—and refused to recombine the parts in any fashion that imposed *meaning*, positive or negative, onto the result: again, the narrow line of the plays' momentary neutrality. The single contemplable presence was the process of change (here deterioration), small-scale units reinforcing the whole at every moment; the plays were effective because of their emptiness. Dramatically, what to do next? After Beckett, serious dramatists, knowing it was impossible to return to Eliot or Camus or Williams, did in fact continue to attempt the experiment. In the main their results were either carbon *Godot*s (the so-called absurd theater) or they were radical theater of the sort mentioned earlier—the off–Off-Broadway movement of the late sixties, a fast-flowering fast-dying phenomenon which produced a kind of activity the best of which was momentarily exciting on the level of cultural revolution; but there were no plays that have lasted.

There may well be no lasting plays for a long time, after Beckett. After Beckett, it is back to basics, back to new combinations built of and reinforced by elements of their own simultaneity: ever more carefully made, and forcing onto the audience an ever greater awareness that the event on stage is theater and not a natural occurrence. As history moves toward such a theater, there may well be valuable dramatic experiences even if there are no lasting plays. A dramatic experience relates to its audience in terms of immediate values. Such a synchronic experience is relatively easily achieved—still rare, but far more common than a new play that will last. The 1971–72 New York season provided one of the few such recent examples, the *Two Gentlemen of Verona* by William Shakespeare/Joseph Papp/John Guare/Galt McDermott.

The material of dramatic presentations will probably be time-bound for a long time, till a consciousness of the kinds of material that are popular for a variety of levels of psychic awareness within a unified political community can develop, a community possibly as large (and, in terms of survival, ultimately necessarily as large) as all the international working class societies. It would in addition be the kinds of material that could transcend the moment in history to which it addresses itself. It is no accident that a call for such a theater sounds like a call for a new Shakespeare, and equally no accident that the best "new" New York play in years should be based on a Shakespeare play—and on one of his weakest at that. The key both to the powerful dramatic experience and to the potential lasting play remains: simultaneity—how much is going on at the same time (not all of which need by any means be recognized consciously). This is not, however, formless simultaneity in the usual multimedia sense, and not in the antiform sense called for by aesthetic anarchists who confuse political revolution with cultural revolution, believing that destruction of old-style bourgeois form in art will lead directly to a chaos after which the political revolution will assert itself. This latter at best serves as negation to calcified cultural institutions. But Beckett has already served much of this purpose, and it has become possible for a vanguard to begin the negation of the negation.

The multimedia event is perhaps the weakest kind of negation. It is still essentially fragmenting, most often a passivity-provoking form, barraging the audience with disorganizing stimuli. It will succeed almost never, and then only when its infinite-number-of-monkeys/infinite-number-of-typewriters accidental-coincidence premise is fulfilled. In virtually every case the result will be chaos. This is not simultaneity. But it can be used to the integration propagandist's ends.

On the other hand, simultaneity can be controlled, and not merely in the sense that all artwork is pre-planned, carefully controlled. Simultaneity can function both within the unique work, and in the relations among any collective of artwork. The texture of Beckett's sense of reality is the microcosm of controlled simultaneity. Though in the content of his work he can be compared to the sterile mule, chomping dry grass and weeds in a technological junkyard, in the presentational texture of his plays (more even than in his novels) he represents, writ small, the possibilities of art in a revolutionary society.

(In accepting this claim one should not see any contradiction with the view of Beckett I expressed above, that in the end his work contributes to the deadening of sensibilities for most of the audience. Beckett's plays have been produced for time-bound audiences, audiences taught to see plays for their content-as-story. His plays will continue to be read, perhaps even played, for audiences also primarily time-bound—but bound to a future moment, when his pieces of content will more clearly be seen as elements from a culture no longer present, hence sufficiently distanceable to allow for a separation between audience involvement and the process of the play. Then the rich simultaneity of the texture will itself become visible, and conscious: no longer sterile, but a potential progenitor of a series of popular art forms.)

To repeat: Beckett's controlled simultaneity suggests the possibilities of (dramatic) art in an age of technological retention. Writ large, simultaneity means the popular (both large-scale and easy) availability of materials (finished products as well as techniques) which can be used by any audience or individual. The work of art, at hand, easily viewable as a piece of history as well as for pleasure, is examinable and ponderable in the sense that fiction was once popularly ponderable before a desire to do so was undercut by film and television. Today, with ever more easily accessible movieolas and small videotape units one can begin to examine and re-examine all forms of electronically viewable experience. A ponderable work of art becomes, increasingly, part of an open communications system. Critique becomes possible when the film ceases to pass by only once before the eyes; the film and the screen cease to dominate over the viewer; the artwork ceases to be controlled by the capitalist who runs the theater or by the television station manager who owns the tools of retention and reproduction. The viewed experience ceases to make the viewer its slave when he can reproduce the experience at (his own) will.

Simultaneity on the level of electronic retention and reproduction means easy access to film libraries, cheap videotape units, information banks, computers for the dissemination of information (rather than for the storage of secret files), penny photocopy units, and the dozens of forms of media units now utilized for the one-way dissemination of partial information; as we have seen earlier, all these media can be turned against central organizations of repression and secrecy by popular pockets of power in search of full information. The importance of such easily available communications equipment is this: whereas movements from cultural to communicational to political revolution have in the past been sequential, it is now beginning to be possible to render all steps of the process simultaneous and interactive. Previously, with control over the media of communication, a system in power could limit the force, and most importantly the speed, of popularly based humanitarian revolutions (religious revolutions, aesthetic revolutions, even political revolutions). Virtually all such revolutions were quickly undercut. What could not be undercut was integrated into the (usually well-preserved) previous power system. A major cause of the failure of such revolutions: the lack of preinformation as to the nature of the changes desired by the revolutionaries. Popular media of information have been, until recently, relatively unsophisticated. The greater sophistication always lay in the hands of those in power. But the power controllers have only a limited ability to retain a hold on information. Information can be manipulated only when it is allowed to exist in limitedly available quantities. The simultaneous presence of information availability would undercut any traditional dialectic of necessary preconditions for political revolution. The situation is analogous to the underdeveloped countries argument, of whether it is necessary for capitalism to precede socialism if a country is to become technologically self-sufficient. With easy access to available information, the possibilities of serious political change toward more organic institutions increase immensely.

The place of artistic processes in such a world of simultaneous possibility then becomes clear. Valid descriptions of reality can be popularly depicted, and subsequently examined, with great care. One need no longer simply be "moved" by great works of, let us say, dramatic art: one can now return, electronically, to the moment at which one was moved, and examine the material reasons, within the work and within the nature of one's own reactions, for that sensation. A stirring model for action can be understood in terms of camera angles, voice inflections, dialogue continuity, and the juxtaposition of content; a decadent model can be critiqued, step by step, and so understood and transcended. A potential disseminator of information needs nothing more than quarter-inch videotape equipment (half-inch being preferable), equipment becoming ever less expensive on the popular market (though still not cheap, however). With the same equipment it becomes quickly possible for individuals to participate in the collective-as-information-collator and to make videotapes for the dissemination of material on a community-wide scale.

Beyond the community, national and international dissemination become possible when available materials reach a critical mass and institutions are developed for their spread and presentation. The key, at all times, is simultaneous availability—the reproduction and retention of materials, the constant possibility of technological training for an increasing number of artisans, some of whom will become artists. The artwork itself, that which is most effective in raising the awareness of its audience—awareness of human possibility, of the possibilities of change altogether—this work will be recognized as achieving its power by microcosmically reproducing the texture of historical social conditions visible through the artwork itself.

Beckett is the last of the modernists, and the first the impact of whose dramatic materials is explicable predominantly in terms of presentational texture. That he speaks primarily of impotence is, for the future, not important; in terms of content it is, in fact, valuable, in Ernst Fischer's sense: "In a decaying society, art, if it is truthful, must also reflect decay. And unless it wants to break faith with social function, art must show the world as changeable. And help to change it."[17] Beckett's work retains cultural junk; but by depicting this material as cultural junk he negates its value. All that remains is the principle of retention, of the necessity of using whatever is there for the purpose of depicting the possibility of change.

Appendix

CONTRADICTION AND DEMYSTIFICATION:

SOME DIRECTIONS FOR FUTURE ANALYSES

It is possible now to begin an outline of one kind of function served by the critical work of the dialectical analyst of literature—the demystification of social contradictions as these are mirrored or symptomized by literary works. Demystification means clarification, and something more as well: demystification suggests that a process, occasionally conscious though more often not, has taken place earlier and has actively confused the nature of a social situation, and its literary depiction, for the benefit of a specific part of a society, a part which turns out to be its dominant class. Beneath this confusion—a confusion usually assumed by various segments of society, all equally propagandized, to be so-called common sense— it is possible for the dominant class within a society to act with relative freedom in the maintenance and furtherance of its interests. Again here the question of explicit malevolent domination is usually peripheral; in a successful hegemonic situation both dominant and dominated classes believe their associations to be normal human relationships, justly and properly determined by a god or by birth or by money. The ideology which functions best for the dominant class, whether or not it is in the best interests of the whole of society, has become and is accepted as the dominant ideology of the whole society. Mystification is the complex of developed processes utilized, again most often nonconsciously, to keep from analysis questions relating to the best interests of this whole society. Karl Mannheim speaks of such mystification as the imposition of certain kinds of false consciousness which "degenerate into ideologies whose function it is to conceal the actual meaning of conduct rather than to reveal it."[1] Demystification is the process of dismantling false though dominant, other- and self-imposed, ideologies.

Contradiction means an opposition, the extremes of which are functions within a larger whole; this larger whole is both spatial and durative in nature. Every event, every movement, every institution has its contradiction, its opposite that may serve also as its complement; in mechanics there is action and reaction, in mathematics plus and minus, in economic society the manufacturing price and the selling price of a commodity. In the finished literary product (in its content as well as in its ideological and formal structure) the reader often sees only one part of a contradiction: the results of authorial choices, made consciously or unconsciously, to present one scene or sentiment or manifestation or juxtaposition, and to suppress another or others which would be in contradiction with those chosen for literary depiction.

There are often clear associations between choices made by an author for the purpose of literary economy—that is, to signal as much information as possible to the reader in as few words as possible—and the perpetuation of unexplored contradictions. Therefore one purpose in the next pages is to begin sorting out programmatically some of the ways the processes of mystification themselves can be brought to visibility, can be depropagandized.

I have been suggesting throughout that an artwork and its critique are interconnected creations. These creations can depict the nature of social contradictions and perhaps as well suggest certain alternative forms of human existence. And such creations can explore the forms and the material of mystification, together with some methods for overcoming contradictions that lie behind mystified segments of human existence. Consequently, a demystifying critique can perhaps make it possible to relate works of art to an improved, a less antagonistically contradictory, future. In this way the literary presentation of human associations can be made to serve, beyond the text, as a catalyst for open social communication. (It is of course possible for writers to pose certain basic contradictions as already resolved, or to resolve such contradictions by means of, for example, a novel's narrative or a developing association among a play's protagonists. The more basic the contradiction, however—that is, the more it is inherent in the very texture of the described or depicted society, of the hegemonic foundations upon which a society has grown and developed—the more difficult it is to resolve the contradiction within or through the literary text alone. Resolved contradictions of this sort are usually superficial contradictions, and their resolution matters little beyond the text itself.)

The antagonistic contradiction then: such a contradiction requires the presence of at least two phenomena or situations grown to palpable existence separately in a fragmented society—earlier or later; in different places; among opposing classes—any two recognized realities which when seen in juxtaposition oppose (though perhaps also complement) each other's intentions, values, goals. It is the function of mystification to obscure the actual fact of contradiction. This, as we have seen, is a process by which internal requirements of the hegemonic society (in our own day, capitalist bourgeois society in the western world, state socialism in the Soviet Union, social democracy in Sweden, and so on) hide the inner workings of antagonistic contradictions from those who suffer most from the perpetuation of these contradictions —in bourgeois capitalism, our own case, this would be the various working classes, those who receive less in compensation than the products of their labor are worth,

and who must not be allowed to recognize they have
been in effect swindled of the creations of their productive powers. The forces of contradiction are exceptionally important phenomena in that they are a stimulus to progress.
Contradictions exist throughout any society. Their recognition, analysis, and resolution most often result in an
improved society (although inevitably new contradictions arise from new conditions). To obscure the fact of
contradiction behind the cosmetics of propaganda only
hides the human problem of which a contradiction is the
symptom. The dominant social class in one way or another creates the prevaricated absence or invisibility of
contradictions because a potential explication and resolution of such contradictions could well cost it money or
power. To take a couple of examples, both at bottom economic: a union claims mine working conditions are un-
safe; the mine owner says safety standards are high;
nothing is done because introducing new safety devices
is expensive. Or: an American president must present
one version, a lie, about his international policy and
about his domestic spying because admission of another
version, journalistically reported and more correct,
would reduce both his prestige and the power that prestige brings with it. An honest resolution of either contradiction and the subsequent progress it could bring
about—decreased mining hazards, or more open government—would be against the owner's or the president's
personal interests. More broadly, because improved safety standards in one mine would result in demands for
safety measures in all mines, and because an open explanation of executive deceit would betray the possibly
illegal and at least unethical structure of intimate economic connections between politics on the highest level
and corporate oligopoly, the resolution of either contradiction would be against the owner's or the president's
class interests.

Engels and Lenin speak of the irreconcilability of in-
terclass antagonisms, and of the national state as a false

enclosure for such class conflict. Not only are the basic
interests of the bourgeoisie and the proletariat contradictory, but the antagonism between them contradicts both
the establishment and the continuing existence of the
national state itself as a potential solution to that antagonism. Propagandistic enclosure of such class tensions can
therefore be viewed as an artificial avoidance of the contradiction, in this case sweeping the mess of contradictory class interests under the rug of state. To the extent
that hegemonic propaganda vaunts the virtue of the national state to the detriment of international social concerns, mystification continues. Less abstractedly, one
can consider internal contradictions in specific geographic units: the false splendor and opulence of Bel
Air is exposed explicitly when, less than a car-hour way,
farmworkers starve. Here a political/geographic area
functions legally and/or spuriously to undermine farm-
worker militancy by attempting to contain blatant class
contradictions within itself, a liberal/conservative arbitrary convergence of people called Southern California.

Historically, such contradictions have often been
avoided—that is, propagandized and so mystified—
through theosophical disclaimers: "Yes, a great deal of
suffering does exist in the world; we can't understand
why it never stops, we're only men, but in the eyes of
God it all has meaning." Incessant integration propaganda of this sort from those basic ideology-forming
institutions, the organized churches of the world together
with their apologists, once served to explain away the
fabulous wealth of the few who were dominant in religious hegemonies to the vast majority of the poor. The
Catholic Church, an earlier example, has sponsored
and/or created a vast body of literature, from Augustine
to the Wakefield Cycle to Claudel and C. S. Lewis, which
remains behind in testimony to the extent of this cosmetic touch.

In our own time, a network of mystifying, obscuring
rhetoric has kept outwardly incomprehensible contradictions from the analyses which would help delineate their

recognizable economic roots and their social and psychological—their cultural—context. The work of Franz Kafka, for example, an early contribution to the analysis of man as a powerless being faced with a hostile hierarchic environment, has been interpreted out of its conception and into pablum; because intrinsic criticism, itself unable to understand both Kafka and its own social and ideological milieu, decorated Kafka's world with the mystifying label "absurd," millions of readers—under-, post-, and non-graduates—have become adequately comfortable with it. That is, millions of readers need no longer try to understand Kafka's analyzed and scrupulously depicted world of very real horrors, because anyone can see they are *absurd*.

An examination, then, of the phenomena literature and contradiction entails the following recognition:

There are vast material contradictions in both the world of daily personal experience and in the larger world of economic institutions which delimit the nature of one's culture and the details of one's personal experience. Let us say, for example, that the largest percentage of a society does not understand the dynamics of a specific area of economic contradiction, class society, and so is free to be exploited by the implications of that contradiction—here, the labor market. In this way, one selected aspect of the contradiction can be made to serve that class of people which has the power consciously or unconsciously to manipulate the whole of the contradiction. It becomes then a major function of literature—the novel, the play, the essay—to depict, describe, and begin thereby to demystify the network of contradictions within a culture and its institutions so that its citizens, in their roles as audiences of dramatic productions and as readers, can begin to understand the places ascribed to each of them within that culture and economy; and, perhaps, to begin changing their imposed roles. Similarly, a major collective function of the scholar/critic is to depict, describe, and so continue the demystification of, these contradictions—within the culture which produced

the work, and with full implications for the scholar/
critic's culture.[2]

There are, generally speaking, three kinds of processes
by which a piece of writing—a piece of literature or a
piece of critique—can help demystify the nature of certain contradictions in the world. (The order of this list-
ing ought not be taken as a value hierarchy of processes.
Rather, it suggests that audiences of differing literary
and ideological awarenesses will be willing to open
themselves to different kinds of literary materials.)

1. A depicted or described *analysis*, by the creator of
   artworks—here the writer—and by the scholar/
   critic, of the antagonistic contradictions in both a
   society and its culture or cultures.
2. A depicted or described tentative *resolution*, by the
   writer *and* by the scholar/critic, of the material content of these antagonistic contradictions.
3. *Action* by the writer *and* by the scholar/critic based
   on that hypothesized resolution, so that its validity
   may be tested and measured, and consequently
   modified.

The scholar/critic who deals with literature in dialectical terms has certain tools which allow him to differen-
tiate among and explain these processes, and to participate at some time in all of them and at all times in as
many as his abilities allow. That is, the various aspects
of such a critic's analyses are continually associated with
their (consciously time-bound) contexts, so that his/her
bases for judgments can be seen, weighed, and possibly
developed by the reader; dialectical analysis, though
necessarily selective, takes as one of its givens a sufficient
explanation of, in Lukacs' term, the *typicality* of the
scene or character or narrative unit in question. So dialectics in criticism helps explain the relationship of a
literary event or structure to its context—the historically
delimited nature of such a relationship, those elements
in the relation which symptomize its typicality—in
order to explicate the primary purposes of the passage

or segments in question. In addition, it recognizes itself to be time-bound, establishing a relation between the text (and its historical moment) and the moment of analysis.[3]

Positivistic criticism, conversely, most often participates in the continuing mystification of the artwork. Such criticism is selective as well, but the nature of its selection processes are usually delimited to one relationship alone, the association between the formal text and the critic's personal, often idealizing, and usually unhistorical and eclectic choices of exemplary material from the text. Much of the conceptualization found in positivistic criticism is therefore more easily based on time-bound critical choices (themselves often contradictory), and consequently contradictions in the texts and in the culture or cultures of a society remain (or worse, become increasingly) mystified.

In the elaboration of these three processes, a unifying concept can be kept in mind: as a demystifier of society, the difference between the scholar/critic and the artist/ writer (who like Diego Rivera paints what he sees and not what John D's grandson Nelson asks him to paint) is in the tools each uses. The ends of the artist who uses his external world as his model and of the scholar/critic are the same, and their tools are complementary. Their successes or their failures can be understood only in terms of the audiences for whom they are writing, painting, analyzing, performing.

Literature is one kind of discourse, one collective sphere, in which to discover, and demystify for others, the nature of social and psychological contradictions as these exist or existed in the world contemporaneous with the artwork. What one normally thinks of as art—a picture, a poem, a formula, a critique, a cathedral— furthers the process of discovery, whether in the so-called arts, or in the social, the physical, and the biological sciences. (That is, the concrete discoveries and descriptions of science, such as that of the double helix, are as primary a statement of the believed nature of human

existence at a given moment in time as in the writing of
The Trial.) Both the artistic/critical and the scientific
imaginations attempt to uncover the material bases for
human existence and then to explain this reality, or parts
of this reality, to their several, sometimes overlapping,
audiences. The similarity between artistic and scientific
inquiry lies in the common humanistic and most often
dialectical search to determine the specifics of the physical basis of existence. In this respect, after Einstein the
methodologies of most of the quantitative sciences are
both positivistic—subscribe to Ellul's version of the myth
of Science—and, in their historical juxtapositioning and
conjunctions, dialectic. That is, scientific research in a
field is built around a model or a series of interdependent
models which can order the information available to that
field. As additional information is accumulated, the
model, or paradigm, is first modified, finally revolutionized. New information, often contradictory in nature,
nearly always forces a reconsideration of previously
accepted norms in a given area, whether in the structure
of the cell wall, in the coding of DNA, or in the nature
of human evolution. Scientific progress has come to accept the pain as well as the necessity of reorganizing its
subdivisions to fit new information, and the functional
truth-value of new paradigms is recognized as a basic
demystifying achievement.[4]
Humanistic progress, too, is capable of the recognition
of new paradigms. But sometimes the complex nature
of the positivistic critic's language—muddy and vague,
or multiform and subtle, a judgment depending on one's
commitment to bourgeois positivism—keeps paradigmatic shifts from coming to early recognition for a contemporary, let alone a popular, audience. Both historically and immediately, the notation of paradigmatic
change in human value-systems is so closely associated
with the description of daily activity and daily existence
that to explain such change in daily language often
leads to vagueness. Part of the task, therefore, of the
dialectics of criticism is to find, or if necessary to create,

the language necessary to describe historically evolved configurations of human institutions and new relationships among these institutions. Here then is a place, within human and social (and so humanist and socialist) progress, for literature, and for scholarship and criticism: to crash each new paradigm—a recognized, analyzed, restructured, in largest terms more correct or exact, description of a society and its culture—into the consciousness of the work's and the critic's audience.

The difference between artistic/scientific and artistic/ humanistic progress has been this: for the artist/scientist the search for the material basis of existence takes place in the material world. The search is continued all the way to fundamental structures. It creates new paradigmatic explanations of existence as it uncovers basic units of reality and discovers associations among these units. (To this extent, that is in its goals, the search is consistent with Ellul's formulation of the myth of Science.) For the western artist/humanist the search for the material basis of existence is also material, but that search, up to the last few years predominantly under the aegis of bourgeois positivism, has rarely been founded in such new analyses as were demanded by historical change. While the least of scientists could in his inquiries stand on the shoulders of giants, the bourgeois humanist was forced back into solitary necessity, into a constant re-examination of his immediate situation and its often oversimplified relation to the object of his examination. Such perspective as he may have had was limited to the "survey of the field."

On the other hand, dialectical tools for demystification allow the scholar/critic (who also surely engages in constant re-examination of the world he/she describes) to comprehend as well the changing base from which his/her analyses are taking place; it thereby becomes possible for makers and readers of critique to understand the role played by critique within the perspective their own history gives to this role. From such a perspective it begins to come clear why it is no accident that the humanistic description of existence (the product of the artist, and of the critic) changes as the relationships within economic and within cultural production change, why it is already cliché to mention that there are economic reasons for the ideological evolution of the novel, for the rise of surrealism and futurism, for the inadequacy of live bourgeois theater: these changes cannot be understood apart from the historical societies out of which these literary descriptions arose.

For the critic the components of historical change as depicted by the work are to be first discerned, then analyzed; the specific limitations of the work can then be understood, and consequently both the literary work and the discourse it brings into being, once demystified, can perhaps be translated into action by their audiences. A great deal of work, certainly: but this may be considered an essential task, collective in nature, of literature and criticism.

There are three processes, then, by which a piece of writing can help in the demystification of both the text and the larger world. The first asks for an *analysis* of social or individual contradictions as depicted in the literary work. Most of the great storytelling novelists and playwrights have done precisely this. They catch up the reading audience with a depiction of contradictions which the reader feels to be omnipresent, in the novel's world and in his own. In this kind of fiction there is little explanation of the action—the action is seen and understood, we say, in the mind's eye, because the description is "so vivid." Historically the good storyteller took part primarily in the first of these processes. To do more would, for the bourgeois reader, have detracted from the story. Jane Austen's country world—small groups of landed gentry, some with aristocratic pretensions, confronting the nineteenth century—stands in clear relief even to an audience of the 1970's; to present apparently trivial details within the great issues of provincial society, she portrays the contradictions between some needs of the human heart and those artificial so-

cial moralities imposed on its citizens by any middle-
class society. Similarly Flaubert, Zola, and Ibsen, from
differing ideological perspectives and with broader
analytic strokes, painted scenes of internal and external
class conflict by structuring social and psychological details in ideologically juxtaposed patterns; and it was
Walter Scott's genius, as Lukacs has explained, to tell
stories which capture worlds from the past by re-creating
social structures out of contradictory narrative details—
class opposition, and the tensions and struggles these
oppositions set in motion—and which form a historical
basis for his characters' strengths and inadequacies. Such
literary works as these have both a naïve veracity, particularly to a large segment of the literary public, the "un-
trained" readership, and a considerable value as docu-
ments that depict past bourgeois societies.

The writer consciously and critically aware of, and
willing to engage in, an explicit analysis of social and
individual contradictions often does so at the peril of
diminished popularity among his bourgeois readers.
Analysis, for the reader in search of escape, gets in the
way of the flow of a story, of the lilt of a lyric; telling
a reader what and how to think has rarely made for
popular fiction. Nonetheless, a number of the most appreciated writers of the western literary tradition have
successfully integrated analytic depiction and explicit
analysis, often through the wit of their style and the
humor of their examples. These examples, when witless
and humorless, may appear extraneous to the reader in
search of narration; these are the long passages in Her-
man Melville and Thomas Mann we have each been
tempted to skip. On the other hand, Balzac, Dickens,
George Eliot, Tolstoi—all could retain their readers.
Their explicit analyses, though often haphazardly placed
in or inadequately integrated into the narrative, probed
surgically into the segments of the society they described.

The charge can be made, however, that their critique
was inadequate, and because it was inadequate it led and

still leads readers to historically limited conclusions. Few writers have ever described the bureaucracy of the courts better than did Dickens in *Bleak House*, or analyzed more carefully the incidents leading to a deathly legal imbroglio. Yet, having descended far into his analysis, Dickens suddenly throws up his arms and claims all social solutions to be impossible. Man's bitter fate can only be alleviated—slightly, sometimes—by individual human decency. Certainly this fate cannot, says Dickens time upon time, be changed basically by eliminating the destructive economic milieu within which it functions. Differently, Balzac in *Illusions perdues* depicts with the clearest detail those social processes leading to the psychological destructions of two young men, a poet and an inventor. Balzac, himself a reactionary royalist, describes anatomically how early industrial capitalist society tears talent and sensitivity to pieces, shows that there is no hiding place from economic and consequently from moral disaster in either the city or the provinces, and concludes that there is no possible reconciliation between goodness and justice in bourgeois society. His analysis still captivates his reader, but he does not follow out the implications of his story, at least those implications visible to a late twentieth century reader.

To elaborate on these implications, to explore them from the perspective of a later moment, is left to the scholar/critic with a knowledge of intervening history. In this respect it is valuable to grasp fully the relationship between literature and the critical discourse which complements it: the work of the great bourgeois writers is not wrong in its analysis, but it may well be incomplete. So it becomes constructive, from perspectives provided by a later moment in history, to complete, not the fine narratives, but the analyses on which these narratives are based. Balzac perceived and described social perversity more clearly than had any of his contemporaries, and with greater precision than would most of his successors. Such description is a first great step in the process toward demystification.

(In the same sense, all literary works are "incomplete," the results of artistic choices made by the author, playwright, screenwriter, director, or other formulator of materials. Reactionary works or, differently, "lesser" literature—paraliterature such as most cowboy and western novels, science fiction, gothic romances, detective novels—can therefore be seen as even more "incomplete" but capable of supplementation by the critic just as readily, though with somewhat different tools, as high literature. In this sense, "lesser" literary works can be exceptionally valuable for analysis as well: they can be "good" or "better" than high literature, for vast numbers of readers as well as for certain critics.[5])

One is forced to speculate, however, on what profound historical effect the work of, say, Balzac might have had if he had been able to carry his depicted analyses to their conclusions—the narrative power of Balzac combined with the analytic ability of, let us say, Marx. (Marx himself had planned an analysis of Balzac.) It has often been easy to scoff at such a unifying possibility by subscribing to that theory of liberal psychology that a person's mind is either synthetic *or* analytic, never both. The either/or fragmentation has been used as the excuse for avoiding total commitment to the implications of their work to which all too often bourgeois writers have paid lip and, self-fulfillingly, mind service. Balzac's or Dickens' analysis stopped short at each of their own historical moments, and so was often destructive even to attempts at reform. For a later time, however, their work provided one prototype for radical social analyses. In this later time, every new analysis had, and has, to be carried out in relation to new social conditions. Balzac's work is supplemented by the history of the critique and explication of his work, within a larger, because later, sense of the specific limitations of his economic and social world, and, for us, within a beginning comprehension of that moment in time to which Balzac's world evolved —our own.

Literary media other than fiction have been necessary,

in a predominantly bourgeois society, to describe the
manner in which contradictions may be resolved. Writers as disparate as John Stuart Mill, Walter Benjamin,
C. Wright Mills, and Leszek Kolakowski chose the essay
as their explicative medium; so of course did Marx. Some
poets, in a lesser because merely formal way, played
with the graphic possibilities of resolution through verse.
Brecht and Shakespeare used the stage.

This then is the second possible process for demystification: a hypothetical *resolution*, by means of theoretical
exploration, of immediate and visible contradictions. The
essay, the most immediate form of written communication, has been an important tool in the process of resolution. It gets to the point, ideally, as quickly as possible,
with decreased intervention of technique, or "art." In a
linear and rational world, the essay has served even
dialectic purposes well, for it quickly reveals muddy-
minded or self-serving mystification. Hard analysis
stands the test of repeated reading. The discourse of an
essay can clarify and overcome contradictions within an
issue by weeding out those elements which have been
made irrelevant by, for example, the passage of time.
That is, in a resolved issue, the description of reality is
consistent with the material elements of the immediate
historical moment or phenomenon which has been analyzed. This is not to suggest that an essay about, let us
say, North American inflation in 1970–75 and a subsequent decline in governmental support to cultural activity will be free of contradictions, for certainly that
period itself was not. Such contradictions as are present
would clearly become part of the *content* of this kind of
essay, because they are part of the world with which
the essay is dealing. To the greatest possible extent, however, these time-bound contradictions would be absent
from the critical ideology which informed such an analysis of inflation/cultural support relationships.

The literature of the stage, the Wakefield Cycle and
Beckett's plays notwithstanding, has also functioned as
a medium for the presentation of the hypotheses of reso-

lution. Its two greatest practitioners, Shakespeare and
Brecht, both lived in periods of primary transition in
social value structures—one at the beginning of Renaissance individualism, the other at its conclusion. Shakespeare was protobourgeois; Brecht, though born into a
late bourgeois world, was protoproletariat. Shakespeare
saw the basic values of his world becoming, at bottom,
egalitarian and individualist. He sensed correctly that
progressive individualism as a value structure was in
strong variance with the hierarchical hegemonic tradition, and so would lie in contradiction with the very real
collective needs of society. Brecht saw the larger value
patterns of his world evolving from the latter moments
of post-Renaissance individualism and its institutions
(late capitalism, linear rationality, imperialism, etc.)
to an as yet unformed communality. Both Shakespeare
and Brecht lived at moments in history during which
the energy of new primary value structures lay in pre-
carious balance and, to them, highly visible contradiction, with the fortified institutions of the old. Eliza-
bethan England: the new individualism both active and
attractive, the old feudal orders listless but still mighty.
Europe after the First World War: the individual as
basic unit of value still pre-eminent; a new sense of
community as the basic unit of human survival becoming apparent. The work of both Shakespeare and Brecht
depicts characters succeeding or failing within the social
and psychological contradictions created by the historical
evolution of value structures in their times. Macheath
and Prospero, Azdak and Imogene transcend immediate
contradictions by opting for a real or forcedly false
utopic image of the future; Baal, Hamlet, Macbeth, Joan
Dark fail in their analyses of the contradictions that
serve as the ideological framework of their plays. For
Shakespeare and for Brecht, the possibilities or impossibilities of an analysis leading to resolution seems to
have been the central issue of their time and so their
basic purpose for writing plays.

    The plays of both Brecht and Beckett portray fragments of human life. Beckett depicts pieces of cultural junk, parts of the end of a world comprised of a previously powerful ideological network. Brecht depicts exploratory bits and pieces, tentative experiments in demystification that can lay the groundwork for the future by showing the revolutionary tendencies of victims, of the jetsam from that same world. This difference between Beckett and Brecht, a difference which determines the form of their plays, grows out of their choices of which fragments to depict. Laying to rest the ghosts of the past is a cleaning-up process; it results in a closed dramatic form, one which requires a supplementary critique. The work of a playwright who examines the tendencies of the future requires of his audience not only a critique of his dramatic analyses and his tentative resolutions but also a series of actions which can make of those depicted tendencies the basis for long-term discourse relating to a more humane social future.

So any form of literature which attempts to depict or describe such tentative resolutions for the contradictions it ponders—Brecht's theater, Marx's polemical essays—must necessarily deal with time. Contradictions are resolved only through the humanly created temporal evolution of (what is later called) one "period" into another, either in the external world (social change), or in the ideology of the protagonist (psychological development), or in both. Hence the historical novel might seem a handy medium through which to depict the processes of resolution were it not that most bourgeois writers of historical fictions have usually turned to the past either to escape from the difficulties of explaining present circumstances, or to validate the confusion of the present by depicting a past world as an ideological carbon copy of the present. Those contemporary narratives which utilize a world of the future have usually been either apocalyptic or fantastic (science) fiction. At its best, science fiction can depict worlds which have transcended the contradictions of contemporary earthly society. To some extent Stanislaw Lem's *Solaris* and Ursula LeGuin's *The*

Left Hand of Darkness and *The Dispossessed* function in this manner (while of course dealing with contradictions arising in and from the world of the narrative). But most science fiction relies on a predictive bourgeois ideology. Ray Bradbury's *Martian Chronicles*, for example, is a reactionary document because he acclaims bourgeois individualism and interplanetary colonialism as a human solution following the destruction of the earth. That is, Bradbury, like many science fiction writers, is incapable of suggesting the form and nature of needed resolutions for a speculated future because he has no clear theoretical grasp of a history with which to posit situations more workable than those dressed-up carbon copies of the present which his narratives depict. It is, in short, necessary for the novelist, as well as for the essayist and playwright, to perceive, analyze, and then to utilize a high degree of historical perspective within a self-conscious dialetics if in their work they are to begin to describe potential or manifest real solutions.

The third part, *actions* to be taken by the writer and critic who deal with alternative ideology, may take a number of forms. It is essential here to understand that the dialectical critic who deals with literature is, most often, a humanist and socialist first; only secondly (professionally) is he or she a literary critic and scholar. For such a critic, analysis and resolution are themselves forms of action. On one side of the contradiction, therefore, it may be necessary for him or her to continue the analysis of the text each explores and of the world each lives in, to broadcast these analyses as widely as possible, and simultaneously to advance the content of research itself. On the other side, action may cause one to stop writing altogether and to participate directly in the daily activities of the world one has described in order to realize the practical implications of one's dialectics.

In most western circumstances the demands of action result in constant re-examination of those depicted literary and those witnessed social situations which can call one's actions into being; the work of a critical dialetics usually moves between these parts of the contradiction, between theorizing and participation. C. Wright Mills continued to teach during the years in which he was writing; like Mills, the writer and the critic can see themselves as educators. And such education need not be considered a phenomenon which takes place primarily in the schools. Education in the seventies can, for example, take place through the processes described earlier, those utilizing, among other media, various forms of the new electronics. Both the highest and the broadest kinds of humanizing/socializing education can result when the tools created by whatever contemporary technology are modified and used for the welfare, not of the majority, but of an entire population. Some writers and critics have discovered, therefore, that it is among their primary responsibilities to learn to control, among others, the electronic media. Brecht the playwright used his stage to educate politically, to depropagandize. He also used his position of "playwright" as a podium from which to educate similarly through media over which he has less control, particularly radio, the open forum, and the essay.

There are, to repeat, at least three processes valuable for the demystification of propagandized images and the equally propagandized network of which they are part. There is nothing inherently superior, one over the other, in the three elements—analysis, tentative resolution, and evaluative action—which comprise this process. But in a given historical context, to a specific historical audience, one process may function better than another. The artistic and critical choice of one process in preference to another, or of some combination of processes, as well as of the idiom through which the presentational discourse takes place, depends on the artist's and critic's assessment of his/her audience's consciousness, at that historical moment. Such an assessment of a propagandized audience can itself begin to help overcome propaganda.

Therefore the example of Brecht serves best to illustrate what I hope is now clearer in its implications: for the artist and for the critic to oppose contemporary integration propaganda, to participate in a process of social demystification, he and she engage fully in all parts of their societies at some time, while at all times they engage in as many parts of their societies as their abilities and their limitations allow. Responsibility for the critic can be defined as participation in a recognition, an analysis, and collective attempts at a resolution, of destructive contradictory circumstances in the world, including the dismantling and rejection of imposed cosmetic mystifications and of those institutions which engender destructive contradictions. The writer and critic barrage his or her communities with a fiction and a critique that help demystify their smaller and larger worlds. Such a process can contribute to social amelioration by bringing about changes in the nature of cultural production and, in conjunction with many others, in relationships within economic production as well.

NOTES

One: Polemical Introduction

1. At the same time, an artwork can satisfy or at least not drive away its audience by providing escape into the universe of wish-fulfillment. That is, while the audience realizes the play is not depicting a valid situation, nonetheless pleasure is created because the audience can for the moment wish it were so. The pleasure of most musical comedy happy endings is of this sort. A recent piece of work on the late nineteenth century melodrama in the U.S. explores theoretical as well as some specific relations between audience needs and the pleasure of watching recognizably false situations depicted on stage (Carol Sweedler, "American Social Melodrama, 1885–1905," Ph.D. diss., University of California, San Diego, 1975).

2. "The Dramatic Process," *Bucknell Review* 19 (Spring 1972): 3–30.

3. "Base and Superstructure in Marxist Cultural Theory," *New Left Review* 82 (November–December 1973): 3–16.

Two: Information, Distortion, Propaganda

1. There may at first appear to be two Jacques Elluls: Ellul the theorist of social/political institutions and Professor of the History of Law and of Social History, teaching at the Université de Bordeaux since 1946; and Ellul the Christian theologian. Aside from *The Technological Society*, trans. John Wilkinson (New York: Knopf, 1964); and *Propaganda: The Formation of Men's Attitudes*, trans. Konrad Kellen and Jean Lerner (New York: Knopf, 1965), to which all page citations in the text refer, he is also the author of *A Critique of the New Commonplaces*, trans. Helen Weaver (New York: Knopf, 1968); *The Political Illusion*, trans. Konrad Kellen (New York: Knopf, 1967); *Metamorphose du bourgeois* (Paris: Calman-Levy, 1967); *Histoire des Institu-*

tions (Paris: Presses Universitaires de France, 1956); among other works. *The Meaning of the City* (Grand Rapids, Mich.: Eerdmans, 1970), trans. Dennis Pardee, is a Christian analysis of urban civilization. Ellul's Christian theology provides him with psychic structures which permeate his social analysis. The two Elluls are very much parts of the same intellect. I should add that the French title of *Propaganda* is, more accurately, the plural, *Propagandes*. In English, propagandas, as a concept, is somewhat clumsy. Nonetheless I shall be using it at times when it is necessary to suggest the simultaneous existence of several sorts of propagandas.

2. It is precisely the complexity of the technological society which calls for propaganda—i.e., controlled partial information from the hegemonic technostructure's power source which asserts the high values of the individual's participation in and subordination to the largest complexes. Were it conceivable to have a technological society which was not complex, specific goal-producing propaganda would not be nearly so important. But when disorganized information is on all sides available to a community, it becomes necessary for each specific arm of a technostructure to direct applicable information to its adherents in order to "deconfuse" them—to show them the proper path, to retain specific controls over them for the technostructure's purposes.

3. Contemporary nonliterate persons are usually enslaved by social and economic conditions. They are ciphers to, and so can be controlled by, their literate masters. But in those few global situations remaining where a people have been forgotten or have never been discovered by technology, McLuhan would still reserve the concept of freedom of mind—such a people would most likely be open to nonlinear, nonrational, and nonliterate stimuli. Even the illiterate member of a society in the early stages of technology could retain this freedom of mind, which in once progressive capitalist terms was read as laziness and irresponsibility, as a lack of goal-orientation on the part of the citizen who by definition was not functioning according to linear values. That is, such persons had not yet learned, e.g., been propagandized into believing, the basics of capitalism.

4. It must not be forgotten that this discussion takes place within the information/propaganda/freedom context, itself only a part of a larger whole. Primitive societies are dominated by structures of their own. Here only one kind of freedom/limitation system is in question, that defined by the use and control of information to present and distort the social mind and the social mind's subsequent control over activity.

5. For Ellul, a technician is one who utilizes "any complex of

standardized means for attaining a predetermined result." Not all technicians are propagandists. A technician produces goods and services for his society; he becomes a propagandist when he begins to proselytize the value of his goods and services. *"Technique,"* says Ellul, *"is the totality of methods rationally arrived at and having absolute efficiency* (for a given stage of development) in *every* field of human activity" (*Technological Society*, p. xxv).

6. One view, and much of the image, of technological societies is that all technological development is linear. By linearity here I mean the *cogito* analysis of man I mentioned above, but translated to technology itself. Unless an analysis of the values which a technology serves is constantly taking place, i.e., if a technology continues to develop itself in automaton fashion without the check of its negative side effects, it will become tangential to the social system it was meant to support and to nourish, and so will be destructive of it. A principle of technology, "If it works, it's good," is (technologically) valid to a point; but when the principle evolves to "If it worked for them (elsewhere, last year, a generation ago—what was good enough for my father, etc.), then it'll work for us," technology starts off on the path toward potential human destruction.

7. I am grateful for these distinctions to Jeffrey Weinstein.

8. By *myth* Ellul means, and I use the term in his sense, those greater structures of the universe which are felt constantly but which would be invisible and ineffable were it not for a man-made abstraction of the structure, the pattern, of the myth. Hence life/death/rebirth, so verbalized, is a constructive mythomorphic pattern, basic to the continuation of a society. Or, on the other hand, the incest taboo myth attempts to negate a destructive social pattern, one which would lead, if it became the dominant pattern, to an ultimate demise of the community. Mythomorphic abstractions are fleshed out by a society for its own ends and in its own idiom. Sunrise/day/sunset can be described as Apollo racing his chariot across the heavens, making the phenomenon less dreadful, less threatening. Oedipus, living out the incest taboo pattern, demands his expulsion from society. Elsewhere, Ellul snubs the idea of evolutionary human history as a reality to be taken seriously. He describes history as a collection of events in which, if one sees a pattern (and he admits many have), it is because one has imposed it: "Nobody doubts that history has a direction. Nobody, that is, except historians! A serious historian is obliged to say, 'That's the way it happened'— period. But somebody who knows nothing about history except what he learned in primary school immediately perceives a thread, a line. The bothersome part is that this line is not always

the same. Clear as day, Michelet saw the direction of history in
the development of freedom. In our day this is no longer exactly
true; and if Hegel is coming back into style, that is no accident!
But how is it that we do not see the incorrigible stupidity of saying that a given event happens because it is in the direction of
history?" (*A Critique of the New Commonplaces*, pp. 30–31). He
opposes a mechanistic Hegel. He does not come to terms with a
materialistically dialectical Marx, one who would never claim
that an event happens because History has willed it, but who
describes the relations between changing economic conditions,
changing ideology, and the events these allow rather than cause.

9. Ellul establishes these categories in *Propaganda* (p. 40), but
does not explore them. It is not his job to do so, he has said
earlier. Here they are central to an examination of the propagandist's ability to embrace *all* in a corporate bourgeois state and
use the pertinent parts of it for his own ends. These secondary
myths are parts of a historical heritage, a tradition which has
evolved over half a thousand years and which remains important
as the material base of western value systems. See also note 10.

10. In much oversimplified and capsule form, the history of
evolving western value systems (that is, those upon which contemporary western ideology is based) can be seen as a movement
from tribal communality in Homeric Greece to the heights of
individualism following Alexander's conquests and through to
republican Rome, then the emergence and dominance of feudal
communality for a Christian millenium, and the reassertion of
individualism in association with the various renaissances, an
individualism that reached its height with nineteenth century
capitalism. Today, in this largest of historical dialectics, there
can be seen a new negation, employing collective values, as individualistic myths and their institutions are undermined and new
myths, many as yet unverbalized, come to dominance. The propagandist helps, often despite himself, to create them and so to control as many of them as possible. For a discussion of these principles as they apply to a practical consideration, the history of
western theater, see my essay "The Dramatic Process."

11. *The Long Goodbye* (Boston: Houghton Mifflin, 1954), p.
286. The example is one of thousands available in popular literature. With Linda Loring, the speaker, a very rich early-middle-
aged woman, the integration propagandist has partially failed.
But in greater part he has succeeded: she is not happy with her
present state, yet she continues to try to satisfy her needs. The
question one has to ask about her is, "What else can she do?" To
answer "Nothing else," is to respond from within her own context: only a meta-analysis of her situation would allow for a different response, and of this Linda Loring, and perhaps Chandler

as well, were incapable. Their incapacity is a sign of the success of the integration propagandist. But in the 1960's precisely Linda Loring's kind of dissatisfaction, allowed to exist as a safety valve for too long, became the basis of a large-scale meta-analysis that resulted in a vast array of credibility gaps. Many a propagandist, also convinced of his own interpretations of information and value systems (according to the unchanging myth of Science), had forgotten that safety valves can become the material basis of reanalysis. See also the concept of leakage, below.

12. At the height of the gray-flannel-suit/junior-executive era, discomfort at the image of their future grew swiftly among middle-class college youth. Nonetheless, most accepted their destiny placidly because the only (propagandistically) offered alternative was the acceptance of complete alienation. To virtually all middle-class B.A.'s this alternative was a dead end, since the propagandist had carefully shaped it as a dead end. The agitation propagandist was saying, "An alternative! A difficult one, perhaps an awful one, but an alternative!" The integration propagandist responded, "Here in the bureaucratic technostructure is reality. Not a great reality, but superior to any alternative. The best we can do for you." The graduating classes agreed. A few dabbled in coffeehouses; men in beads and jeans, women in black tights, and folk-singing groups served as momentary titillations; Greenwich Villages the world over prospered. No one challenged the hegemony. During the day, in the light of reason, the commuter train was safer and more comfortable. For a while the bourgeois propagandist had won.

13. Expansionism in nineteenth century terms (late imperialism, manifest destiny) was an essential element in the growth of nationalism. Without expansion, nationalism's subservience to capitalism would soon have become popularly visible. The economic determinant in growth supersedes the national one. Hence national systems were allowed (even fostered, as an opiate very similar in intent to the drugs/alcohol/religion syndrome) by the emerging industrial estate. The economic contradictions within the national state were immediately obvious, but as in the story about the emperor's new clothes, few spoke up. If one had accepted nationalism as a form enclosing like and like, then the resulting European nations were most often ludicrous conglomerates, and the African and Asian colonies were economically determined arbitrary manipulations. What if West Africa was comprised of coastal, rain forest, and plains people? For competing European expansionists, it was far more important that each control masses of fertile land and have access to a good harbor, no matter how tribes had to be split up. The imposed idea of the national colonies, many of which were sanctified as nations

in the mid-twentieth century when the myth of the Nation had already long fallen from its previous vaunted position, is a late absurdity among the contradictions of expansionist imperialism. Yet nationalistic freedom from colonial rule was the only form of self-determination which many colonized people had been taught to consider. They had been propagandized into nationalism. As a result, many of their nations were doomed to unnecessary chaos. The propagandist would point with glee at the failures of these new nations: they were more interested in fighting among themselves than they were in proper democratic government. In addition he could speak in terms of the nationalistic I-told-you-so in order to buttress his state's psychic well-being and superiority, and so overcome much internal confusion, doubt, and uncertainty.

14. The term *technostructure* is John Kenneth Galbraith's and I use it here to place in relief that part of the technological hegemony responsible for corporate planning. Galbraith explains, in that excellent liberal study (which preceded his public conversion to socialism) *The New Industrial State* (Boston: Houghton Mifflin, 1967), that the technostructure "embraces all who bring specialized knowledge, talent or experience to group decision making. This, not the management, is the guiding intelligence—the brain—of the enterprise" (p. 82).

15. There are one or two examples of complex simultaneity on television. The Public Broadcast System's "Electric Company," the program which ironically teaches children to read, takes as one of its principles the idea that the TV screen is not only a picture window to the world, but it is also a canvas on which to paint. This acceptance of the screen as a two-dimensional reality would revolutionize one whole side of the concept of television. For other examples, including the television monitor as a sending as well as receiving unit, see Hans Magnus Enzensberger, "The Consciousness Industry," *New Left Review* 64 (November–December 1970): 13–39, and chapter five of this book.

16. Enzensberger, in "The Consciousness Industry," pp. 13–14, provides a good partial list of those media uncontained by a controlling theory: news satellites, color television, cable relay television, cassettes, videotapes, videotape recorders, videophones, stereophony, laser techniques, electrostatic reproduction processes, electronic high-speed printing, composing and learning machines, microfiches with electronic access, printing by radio, time-sharing computers, data banks.

17. The best form of such a broadcast might well be through the media now controlled by the hegemony. The public at large trusts, in fact relies on, these media. The hegemony's institutions will in most likelihood not allow such a large-scale broadcasting

process to take place. The other way is underground. "Underground" in a mass technological society is coming to mean everything discoverable mainly through the medium of print, through the vast array of printed information. Clearly this is a formidable piece of work, far too large for any individual. Collectivity and collaboration are necessary, if possible using electronic media for dissemination and communication of information.

18. Enzensberger, in "The Consciousness Industry," has attempted to construct the beginnings of such a theory. A passage from his introductory remarks bears repeating:

The new media are egalitarian in structure. Anyone can take part in them by a simple switching process. The programmes themselves are not material things and can be reproduced at will. In this sense the electronic media are entirely different from the older media like the book or the easel painting, the exclusive class character of which is obvious. Television programmes for privileged groups are certainly technically conceivable—closed circuit television—but run counter to the structure. Potentially the new media do away with all educational privileges and thereby with the cultural monopoly of the bourgeois intelligentsia. This is one of the reasons for the intelligentsia's resentment against the new industry. As for the "spirit" which they are endeavouring to defend against "depersonalization" and "mass culture," the sooner they abandon it the better. (P. 20)

19. Nor is Ellul's Aristotelian Christian pessimism helpful.

Man was made to do his daily work with his muscles; but see him now, like a fly on flypaper, seated for eight hours, motionless at a desk. Fifteen minutes of exercise cannot make up for eight hours of absence. The human being was made to breathe the good air of nature, but what he breathes is an obscure compound of acids and coal tars. He was created for a living environment, but he dwells in a lunar world of stone, cement, asphalt, glass, cast iron and steel. The trees wilt and blanch among sterile stone facades. Cats and dogs disappear little by little, going the way of the horse. Only rats and men remain to populate a dead world. Man was created to have room to move about in, to gaze into far distances, to live in rooms which, even when they were tiny, opened out on fields. See him now, enclosed by the rules and architectural necessities imposed by overpopulation in a twelve by twelve closet opening out on any anonymous world of city streets. (*Technological Society*, p. 321)

Such pessimism, here and in other similar passages, plays completely into the hands of the oppressive elements of technological societies and itself constitutes a piece of integration propaganda of the so-what's-the-use sort.

Three: Theaters of Propaganda

1. "Vergnügungstheater oder Lehrtheater?" in *Brecht on Theatre*, ed. and trans. John Willett (New York: Hill and Wang, 1964), p. 73; *Gesammelte Werke 15: Schriften zum Theater I*, ed. Werner Hecht (Frankfurt am Main: Suhrkamp, 1967), pp. 262–272. Brecht's sense of the concept "science" must not be confused with Ellul's.

2. "Problems of Socialist Art," in *Radical Perspectives in the Arts*, ed. Lee Baxandall (Baltimore: Penguin, 1972), p. 215; reprinted from *Labour Monthly* 43 (March 1961): 135–143.

3. Paul A. Baran and Paul M. Sweezy, *Monopoly Capital: An Essay on the American Economic and Social Order* (New York: Monthly Review Press, 1968), p. viii.

4. These last four lines appear only in the English version of the play by Eric Bentley, in *The Jewish Wife and Other Short Plays* (New York: Grove, 1965), p. 104.

5. For example, Ursula LeGuin's *The Dispossessed* (1974) analyzes the social processes of an anarchic society and contrasts such a society with bourgeoisie prevailing elsewhere.

Four: Class Struggle and Late-Medieval Integration Propaganda in the Wakefield Mystery Cycle

1. All citations and translations are from *The Wakefield Mystery Plays*, ed. Martial Rose (New York: Norton, 1961). I have used Rose's edition primarily for its general availability, for its accessibility to a lay reader both in his search for a complete edition of the plays and, when found, for his easier access to the language of the plays. Though Rose's text is a production translation, its few inaccuracies have little if any effect on my argument. A. C. Cawley's thorough *The Wakefield Pageants in the Towneley Cycle* (Manchester: Manchester University Press, 1958) contains the six pageants known as the Wakefield group, as well as an excellent bibliography of other scattered available translations.

2. Marc Bloch, in *Feudal Society: Social Classes and Political Organization*, vol. 2, trans. L. A. Manyon (Chicago: University of Chicago Press, 1964), p. 353, dates the concept *bourgeois*, one

who lives and functions as a merchant or craftsman in an urban area, from the eleventh century. Bourgeois life in any large way did not really begin, however, until well into the fourteenth century. And for the purposes of this examination it is very important not to confuse bourgeois society with capitalism. Ernest Mandel, in *An Introduction to Marxist Economic Theory* (New York: Pathfinder Press, 1970), is careful to distinguish between the presence of capital and the life of capitalistic society, noting that "capital is far older than the capitalist mode of production. The former goes back some 3,000 years, whereas the latter is barely 200 years old." City life need not mean capitalism. The term *bourgeois*, Bloch says, "was employed in unequivocal opposition to the words knight, cleric, villein." There had of course "always existed isolated nuclei of merchants and craftsmen," but from the eleventh century on they "came to be recognized as a distinctive group in society," partly because they lived in towns.

For specific contexts, see Sir John Clapham, *A Concise Economic History of Britain: From the Earliest Times to 1750* (Cambridge: At the University Press, 1949), pp. 105–110; Fritz Rörig, *The Medieval Town* (Berkeley and Los Angeles: University of California Press, 1969), pp. 161–180, for an analysis of urban institutions; and Henri Pirenne, *Medieval Cities* (Princeton: Princeton University Press, 1952, 1969), pp. 130–167, for a discussion of middle-class city life.

3. See Bloch's discussion (*Feudal Society*, pp. 316–319) of the decay of the code of chivalry, though chivalry as the ideal was never truly achieved. Yet the concept of chivalry was retained by conservatives as the golden age, the pinnacle, from which evil new individual values were carrying society down into chaos. See also the discussion of the Wakefield "Abel," below (note 17).

4. *Early Writings*, ed. T. B. Bottomore (New York: McGraw-Hill, 1964), pp. 27–29.

5. The economic context within which the mystery plays developed is of course very important. For my present purposes it is, however, sufficient to note that the fast growth of the wool and cloth industries in the second half of the fourteenth century made Wakefield a major and increasingly wealthy trade center. Though Wakefield was no vast urban cog, nonetheless it attracted the surrounding population for economic and religious reasons; producers and merchants in Wakefield were in direct contact with European wool importers and supplied the needs of other parts of England. Such economic circumstances might well serve as the basis, for example, for arguments that link the vibrant immediacy of detail in the two shepherds' plays with the authors' and the productions' familiarity with the early days of the wool

trade. But again, this sort of question is only peripheral to my intentions here. For additional economic background, M. M. Posten's *The Medieval Economy and Society: An Economic History of Britain in the Middle Ages* (London: Weidenfeld and Nicolsen, 1972), pp. 193–195 ff., is valuable, as is the earlier and more specific though somewhat dated work by Eileen Power, *The Wool Trade in English Medieval History* (Oxford: Oxford University Press, 1941).

6. For a closer examination of the relation between dramatic and religious forms, see Eleanor Prosser, *Drama and Religion in the English Mystery Plays* (Stanford: Stanford University Press, 1961).

7. Varied presentation serves my purposes best, but such variety should not suggest that the Wakefield Cycle is dramatically the best of the extant cycles. "Best" brings the question, best for whom? or for what? I shall deal with this qestion below. By varied I mean more of Hans-Jürgen Diller's conception, that the Wakefield plays present the dramatization of a series of processes, that they do not merely depict a result: "In *Chester* we observe the result, in *Towneley* the process, of thought. But this distinction is only the symptom of a larger one, which is a basic difference in character conception . . . [The *Chester* Herod's] evil disposition is merely described, it does not reveal itself . . . In *Towneley* the abstract concept of evilness is broken down into a number of subquantities which are conveyed to us by Herod's behavior: he is selfish, vengeful, treacherous and violent" ("Craftsmanship of the Wakefield Master," *Anglia* 83 [1965]: 279). And a basic difference in character conception is itself a symptom of something larger—of the increasing importance of both the concept of character as individuation, and the values by which a character may live.

8. See G. R. Owst's long discussion, *Literature and Pulpit in Medieval England,* rev. ed. (New York: Barnes and Noble, 1961), pp. 210–470.

9. Allardyce Nicoll, *Masks, Mimes and Miracles* (New York: Harcourt Brace, 1931, 1963), pp. 135–150; and also Benjamin Hunningher, *The Origin of the Theater* (Hague: Nyhoff, 1955).

10. Prosser (*Drama and Religion,* p. 96) makes a fine case for the absolute interconnection between religious and secular elements in the Wakefield Cycle, concluding of the playwright, that he "could certainly not turn his religious perspective on and off at will." In the same manner, he could not turn on or off at will his economic predilections and his social uncertainties.

11. Diller, "Craftsmanship of the Wakefield Master," p. 273.

12. "Origin of the *Second Shepherds' Play*: A New Theory," *Quarterly Journal of Speech* 52 (1966): 47–57.

13. Prosser, for example, argues (*Drama and Religion*, pp. 184–185) convincingly against such limited views among her predecessors, from Edwin Norris, ed. and trans., *The Ancient Cornish Drama*, 2 vols. (Oxford: Clarendon, 1859), to Hardin Craig, *English Religious Drama of the Middle Ages* (Oxford: Clarendon, 1955). Father F. C. Gardiner's *Mysteries End* discusses the legal and political pressures to cease production of the cycles. He believes Wakefield lost production rights in 1576.

14. Much of the subsequent methodology, examining a work of art in sociological and historical-anthropological terms, is borrowed from procedures developed by the German Marxist sociologist T. W. Adorno. In English his work is available, in sampler fashion, in *Prisms*, trans. Samuel and Shierry Weber (London: Neville Spearman, 1967), dealing primarily with the sociology of music; in *The Jargon of Authenticity*, trans. K. Tarnowsky and F. Will (London: Routledge and Kegan Paul, 1973); in *Negative Dialectics*, trans. E. B. Ashton (London: Routledge and Kegan Paul, 1973); in *Minima Moralia*, trans. E. F. N. Tephcott (London: New Left Books, 1974); and in isolated pieces, including "Theses on the Sociology of Art," trans. Brian French, *Working Papers in Cultural Studies* 2 (Spring 1972): 121–128, from which I excerpt the following (121–123):

> Sociology of art, according to the meaning of the words, embraces all aspects of the relationship between art and society. It is impossible to restrict it to any single aspect, such as the social effects of works of art. This effect is itself only a moment in the totality of that relationship . . . the effects depend on innumerable mechanisms of distribution, of social control and authority, and finally on the social structure, within which the determining relations can be ascertained. They also depend on the socially conditioned level of consciousness or unconsciousness of those on whom the effect is being exercised . . . The ideal of the sociology of art would be to relate objective analysis, that is analyses of the works, analyses of the structural and specific communication networks, and analyses of the subjective findings which can be recorded.

It is within such a network that the Wakefield Cycle should be seen to function.

15. "Pilate—Os Malleatoris," *Speculum* 36 (1961): 308–311.

16. Even in *The First Shepherds' Play* there are clear economic causes for the shepherds' distresses, causes related specifically to late-medieval social factors and not factors pertaining to the time of Jesus; these are, however, more craftfully integrated into the structure of *The Second Shepherds' Play*.

17. "Theme and Irony in the Wakefield 'Mactacio Abel,' "

PMLA 80 (1965): 515–521. In speaking of the contrast between Cain and Abel, Gardner says, ". . . the feudal interdependence of all stations within the scheme of plenitude is based upon the lore of lord for vassal and vassal for lord (as Abel knows), not upon obligation or debt" (516). He goes on to characterize the nature of Cain's despair: "Despair is the inevitable effect of Cain's original substitution of the law of debt for the law of love." Similarly, the soldiers have long since taken the law of debt as their own. When, for example, Herod promises them each a maid, the First Soldier responds, "So long have ye said, but unpaid is the bill!" (275).

18. They come to belief all the more to the advantage of the hegemony because they are convinced by a woman whom they have chided for *being a woman*; in some of the most blatant antiwoman lines in the Cycle, Paul says (489):

> And it is written in our law
> No woman's judgement hold in awe,
> Nor too quickly show belief,
> For with their cunning and their guile
> They can laugh then weep awhile,
> When nothing gives them grief.

Then when Mary is proven correct—by the appearance of Jesus himself—the play makes explicit the Church's acceptance of women as equally capable of having a soul worth saving.

19. That is, knowledge of the sort that penetrates the mystery of understanding paradoxes by accepting them as two parts of a more transcendent truth. "He holds all things in his hand," says an angel toward the end of the *Ascension* play, "No living thing may him withstand, / Then marvel not but understand" (515). This understanding can be delivered only over a period of time. And time is a phenomenon of which self-propagandized communal passive Christian ideology thought it had a sufficiency, even as the concrete economic basis for the thinking of its theorists was turning against them.

20. *Eros and Civilization* (New York: Random House, 1955), pp. 58, 74–75.

21. The analogy is to a great extent sexual; sexual titillation functions whenever sexuality itself is repressed by the mores of the social order, as for example in the average Protestant state.

22. See Sigurd Burkhardt's discussion of how anachronism in a historical play signifies the playwright's attempt to manipulate his audience's reactions. In *Julius Caesar*, for example, Shakespeare used anachronism to relate his plays to the immediate concerns of the audience; he was not simply depicting a historical circumstance ("How Not To Murder Caesar," in *Shakespear-*

ian Meanings [Princeton, N.J.: Princeton University Press, 1969], pp. 3–21).

23. *The Development of Dramatic Art* (New York: Appleton, 1937), p. 168. Choosing judgments made nearly thirty years ago helps underline the historically limited perspective of such criticism.

24. Latin plays little part in the Wakefield Cycle. Pilate at the beginning of *The Talents* (431–438) rants on in Latin, presumably for comic effect; Jesus in *The Deliverance of Souls* speaks only Latin in his early utterances in the underworld, presenting (in the time of the tale) the future language of the Church. Jesus' Latin serves to challenge evil; Pilate's suggests the dangers inherent in using holy language for personal ends.

25. Prosser, *Drama and Religion*, p. 6.

Five: Samuel Beckett and Dramatic Possibilities in an Age of Technological Retention

1. "Seven Notes on *Waiting for Godot*," trans. Leonard C. Pronko, reprinted from *Primer Acto*, no. 1 (April 1957) in *Casebook on Waiting for Godot*, ed. Ruby Cohn (New York: Grove, 1967), pp. 101–107. The cited passage appears on page 103.

2. Beckett, *Proust* [including *Three Dialogues*] (London: Calder and Boyars, 1963), p. 84. Edition cited throughout.

3. For a far more complete analysis according to this model of the fiction of Beckett and a larger description of this model itself, as well as a close analysis of *Krapp's Last Tape* according to the model, see my *Narrative Consciousness* (Austin: University of Texas Press, 1972).

4. Appropriately, the pattern also accommodates the structure of Beckett's career as a writer: struggle to success as a novelist; the novel as an impossible genre; struggle to render playwriting the proper genre for expression (with decreased productivity; the impossibility of anyone writing traditional theater after Beckett's still traditional theater—including Beckett); and the deterioration of the Cartesian writer.

5. See, for an exemplary paradigm of this method, Lucien Goldmann, *Le Dieu Caché* (Paris: Gallimard, 1959), pp. 56–57, fn.

6. Lawrence E. Harvey was the first to note, in any kind of organized way, this process in *Waiting for Godot*. "Art and the Existential in *Waiting for Godot*," *PMLA* 75, no. 1 (March 1960): 137–146. Josephine Jacobsen and William R. Mueller first suggested the dominating existence of a similar pattern, in all

Beckett's works, in *The Testament of Samuel Beckett* (New York: Hill and Wang, 1964.
  7. All citations from *Endgame* (New York: Grove, 1958).
  8. For example, Genevieve Serran, "Beckett's Clowns," in *Casebook on Waiting for Godot*, p. 173: "Gogo systematically doubts; he is totally immersed in a kind of nightmare of nothingness in which everything = everything (nothing = nothing), and he thus erodes the few striking certain ties to which Didi clings." The *Casebook* contains some of the best analysis done on Beckett's work. It also contains a great deal of the most breathless. As an overall document exemplifying the impotence of critical eclecticism, it is first-rate and could itself be made subject to study.
  9. Herbert Marcuse makes a similar argument in *Counterrevolution and Revolt* (Boston: Beacon Press, 1972), pp. 79–80. He recognizes the sequence from cultural to communicational revolution but limits his sense of revolutionary media communication to the traditional art forms—plastic and visual depiction, literature, music—and to "the folk tradition (black language, argot, slang)." These are only beginnings.
  10. Darko Suvin, "Preparing for Godot—or the Purgatory of Individualism," *Tulane Drama Review* (*TDR*) 11, no. 4, T36 (Summer 1967): 23–36; reprinted in *Casebook*, ed. Cohn, pp. 121–132.
  11. For an explanation of this sidelight of dramatic history, see Georg Lukacs, *Goethe and His Age*, trans. Robert Anchor (New York: Grosset and Dunlap, 1969). Lukacs' line of argument, especially in his discussion of the Age of Goethe as Germany's only renaissance, suggests that even a lately unified German state still retained its principalities (*länder*) as basic political units, which in turn retained their semiunique cultural characteristics. The theater would be central to this sense of independence within unity.
  12. Popular in the sense of *easy*. A person who engages in a daily alienating job will not strain himself or herself after it is completed for the day or for the week. Television is easier than film, going to a film is easier than reading a novel.
  13. Walter Benjamin, "The Work of Art in the Age of Mechanical Reproduction," in his *Illuminations* (New York: Schocken, 1969), p. 227. Benjamin wrote (originally in 1936), "Earlier much futile thought had been devoted to the question of whether photography is an art. The primary question—whether the very mention of photography had not transformed the entire nature of art—was not raised. Soon the film theoreticians asked the same ill-considered questions with regard to the film. . . ."
  14. See, for example, Brecht's 1932 speech on the function of radio, "Der Rundfunk als Kommunikationsapparat," in *Gesam-*

melte Werke 18: *Schriften zur Literature und Kunst I,* ed.
Werner Hecht (Frankfurt am Main: Suhrkamp, 1967), pp.
127–134.
  15. It is valuable here to recall Ellul's description (*Propaganda,* pp. 25–32) of the disjunction between information and
the response it brings about, in terms of outer visible action.
Information must reach a point of supersaturation before it can
bring about action on an individual or large-scale level.
  16. I mean in the sense suggested by Ernst Fischer in *The
Necessity of Art,* trans. Anna Bostock (Baltimore: Penguin,
1963): "An artist's subjectivity does not consist in his experience
being fundamentally different from that of others of his time or
class, but in its being stronger, more conscious, and more concentrated" (p. 46).
  17. Ibid., p. 48.

Appendix: Contradiction and Demystification

  1. Karl Mannheim, *Ideology and Utopia: An Introduction to
the Sociology of Knowledge,* trans. Louis Wirth and Edward Shils
(New York: Harcourt, Brace and World, 1936), p. 95.
  2. This series of associated relationships has been a major concern of Marxist criticism from the earliest writings on aesthetics
of Georg Lukacs to, more recently, such works as Fredric
Jameson's *Marxism and Form: Twentieth-Century Dialectical
Theories of Literature* (Princeton: Princeton University Press,
1971), and Jeremy Hawthorn's *Identity and Relationship*
(London: Lawrence and Wishart, 1972).
  3. Jameson, in *Marxism and Form,* explains the tools of dialectical criticism (p. 45) in this way:

The dialectical method is precisely this preference for the concrete totality over the separate, abstract parts. Yet it is more
complicated than any objective apprehension of a merely external kind of totality, such as takes place in the various scientific disciplines. For in these the thinking mind itself remains
cool and untouched, skilled but unselfconscious, and is able to
forget about itself and its own thought processes while it sinks
itself wholly in the content and problems offered it. But dialectical thinking is a thought to the second power, a thought
about thinking itself, in which the mind must deal with its
own thought process just as much as with the material it works
on, in which both the particular context involved and the style
of thinking suited to it must be held together in the mind at
the same time.

4. For a clear discussion of the dialectics of scientific discovery, see Thomas Kuhn, *The Structure of Scientific Revolutions* (Chicago: University of Chicago Press, 1962).

5. I have argued this more extensively in my essay "On the Political Rhetoric of our Narrative Tastes," *Massachusetts Review* 18, no. 1 (Spring 1977): 35–50.

SELECTED BIBLIOGRAPHY

Adorno, T. W. *Aesthetische Theorie.* Frankfurt: Suhrkamp Verlag, 1970.
——. *The Jargon of Authenticity.* Trans. K. Tarnowsky and F. Will. London: Routledge and Kegan Paul, 1973.
——. *Minima Moralia.* Trans. E. F. N. Tephcott. London: New Left Books, 1974.
——. *Negative Dialectics.* Trans. E. B. Ashton. London: Routledge and Kegan Paul, 1973.
——. *Philosophie der neuen Musik.* Frankfurt: Europäische Verlagsanstalt, 1958.
——. *Prisms.* Trans. Samuel and Shierry Weber. London: Neville Spearman, 1967.
——. "Theses on the Sociology of Art." Trans. Brian French. *Working Papers in Cultural Studies* 2 (Spring 1972): 121–128.
Baran, Paul A., and Paul M. Sweezy. *Monopoly Capital: An Essay on the American Economic and Social Order.* New York: Monthly Review Press, 1968.
Baxandall, Lee. *Marxism and Aesthetics: An Annotated Bibliography.* New York: Humanities Press, 1968.
——, ed. *Radical Perspectives in the Arts.* Baltimore: Penguin, 1972.
Beckett, Samuel. *Endgame.* New York: Grove, 1958.
——. *Krapp's Last Tape.* New York: Grove, 1960.
——. *Proust* [including *Three Dialogues*]. London: Calder and Boyars, 1963.
Benjamin, Walter. *Illuminations.* Ed. and with introduction by Hannah Arendt. Trans. H. Zohn. New York: Schocken, 1969.
——. *Versuche über Brecht.* Edited and with introduction by Rolf Tiedeman. Frankfurt: Suhrkamp Verlag, 1966.
——. "The Work of Art in the Age of Mechanical Reproduction." In his *Illuminations.* New York: Schocken, 1969.
Berger, John. "Problems of Socialist Art." *Labour Monthly* 43 (March 1961): 135–143.
Bloch, Marc. *Feudal Society: Social Classes and Political Organization.* Vol. 2. Trans. L. A. Manyon. Chicago: University of Chicago Press, 1964.

Bottomore, T. B., ed. *Karl Marx: Early Writings*. New York: McGraw-Hill, 1964.

Brecht, Bertolt. *Brecht on Theatre*. Ed. and trans. John Willett. New York: Hill and Wang, 1964.

————. "Der Rundfunk als Kommunikationsapparat" [1932 speech on the function of radio]. In *Gesammelte Werke* 18: *Schriften zur Literatur und Kunst I*, ed. Werner Hecht, pp. 127–134. Frankfurt am Main: Suhrkamp, 1967.

————. *The Jewish Wife and Other Short Plays*. Trans. Eric Bentley. New York: Grove, 1965.

————. "Vergnügungstheater oder Lehrtheater?" In *Gesammelte Werke* 15: *Schriften zum Theater I*, pp. 262–272. Frankfurt am Main: Suhrkamp, 1967.

Burkhardt, Sigurd. "How Not To Murder Caesar." In *Shakespearian Meanings*, pp. 3–21. Princeton: Princeton University Press, 1969.

Burns, Elizabeth and Tom, eds. *Sociology of Literature and Drama*. Harmondsworth, Middlesex: Penguin, 1973.

Caudwell, Christopher. *Illusion and Reality*. New York: Russell and Russell, 1955.

Cawley, A. C. *The Wakefield Pageants in the Towneley Cycle*. Manchester: Manchester University Press, 1958.

Chandler, Raymond. *The Long Goodbye*. Boston: Houghton Mifflin, 1954.

Clapham, Sir John. *A Concise Economic History of Britain: From the Earliest Times to 1750*. Cambridge: At the University Press, 1949.

Cohn, Ruby, ed. *Casebook on Waiting for Godot*. New York: Grove, 1967.

Craig, Hardin. *English Religious Drama of the Middle Ages*. Oxford: Clarendon, 1955.

Davis, R. G. *The San Francisco Mime Troupe: The First Ten Years*. Palo Alto, Calif.: Ramparts, 1975.

Demetz, Peter. *Marx, Engels and the Poets*. Trans. J. L. Sammons. Chicago: University of Chicago Press, 1967.

Diller, Hans-Jürgen. "Craftsmanship of the Wakefield Master." *Anglia* 83 (1965).

Ellul, Jacques. *A Critique of the New Commonplaces*. Trans. Helen Weaver. New York: Knopf, 1968.

————. *Histoire des Institutions*. Paris: Presses Universitaires de France, 1956.

————. *The Meaning of the City*. Trans. Dennis Pardee. Grand Rapids, Mich.: Eerdmans, 1970.

————. *Metamorphose du bourgeois*. Paris: Calman-Levy, 1967.

————. *The Political Illusion*. Trans. Konrad Kellen. New York: Knopf, 1967.

———. *Propaganda: The Formation of Men's Attitudes.* Trans. Konrad Kellen and Jean Lerner. New York: Knopf, 1965.

———. *The Technological Society.* Trans. John Wilkinson. New York: Knopf, 1964.

Enzensberger, Hans Magnus. "The Consciousness Industry." *New Left Review* 64 (November–December 1970): 13–39.

Fischer, Ernst. *Art against Ideology.* Trans. Anna Bostock. Harmondsworth, Middlesex: Penguin, 1969.

———. *The Necessity of Art: The Marxist Approach.* Trans. Anna Bostock. Baltimore: Penguin, 1963.

Galbraith, John Kenneth. *The New Industrial State.* Boston: Houghton Mifflin, 1967.

Gardner, John. "Theme and Irony in the Wakefield 'Mactacio Abel.'" *PMLA* 80 (1965): 515–521.

Goldmann, Lucien. *Le Dieu Caché.* Paris: Gallimard, 1959.

———. *Pour une sociologie du roman.* Paris: Gallimard, 1964.

Gramsci, Antonio. *Selections from the Prison Notebooks.* Ed. and trans. Quintin Hoare and Geoffrey Nowell Smith. New York: International, 1971.

Harvey, Lawrence E. "Art and the Existential in *Waiting for Godot.*" *PMLA* 75, no. 1 (March 1960): 137–146.

Hauser, Arnold. *The Social History of Art.* New York: Knopf, 1951.

Hawthorn, Jeremy. *Identity and Relationship.* London: Lawrence and Wishart, 1972.

Hunningher, Benjamin. *The Origin of the Theater.* Hague: Nyhoff, 1955.

Jacobsen, Josephine, and William R. Mueller. *The Testament of Samuel Beckett.* New York: Hill and Wang, 1964.

Jameson, Fredric. *Marxism and Form: Twentieth-Century Dialectical Theories of Literature.* Princeton: Princeton University Press, 1971.

Johnson, Wallace. "Origin of the *Second Shepherds' Play*: A New Theory." *Quarterly Journal of Speech* 52 (1966): 47–57.

Knights, L. C. *Drama and Society in the Age of Johnson.* London: Chatto and Windus, 1937.

Kuhn, Thomas. *The Structure of Scientific Revolutions.* Chicago: University of Chicago Press, 1962.

LeGuin, Ursula K. *The Dispossessed.* New York: Harper and Row, 1974.

Lukacs, Georg. *Die Theorie des Romans.* Neuwied: Luchterhand, 1962.

———. *Goethe and His Age.* Trans. Robert Anchor. New York: Grosset and Dunlap, 1969.

———. *The Historical Novel.* Trans. H. and S. Mitchell. London: Merlin, 1962.

218   *Selected Bibliography*

———. *Probleme des Realismus*. Berlin: Aufbau Verlag, 1955.
———. *Schriften zur Literatursoziologie*. Ed. P. Ludz. Neuwied: Luchterhand, 1961.
———. *Studies in European Realism*. Trans. Edith Bone. New York: Grosset and Dunlap, 1964.
Macheray, Pierre. *Pour une théorie de la production littéraire*. Paris: Maspéro, 1970.
Maltman, Sister Nicholas. "Pilate—Os Malleatoris." *Speculum* 36 (1961): 308–311.
Mandel, Ernest. *An Introduction to Marxist Economic Theory*. New York: Pathfinder Press, 1970.
Mannheim, Karl. *Ideology and Utopia: An Introduction to the Sociology of Knowledge*. Trans. Louis Wirth and Edward Shils. New York: Harcourt, Brace and World, 1936.
Mao Tse-tung. "On Contradiction." In *Selected Works*, 5 vols., 2:13–53. New York: International, 1954–1962.
Marcuse, Herbert. *Counterrevolution and Revolt*. Boston: Beacon Press, 1972.
———. *Eros and Civilization*. New York: Random House, 1955.
———. *Negations*. Boston: Beacon Press, 1968.
———. *One-Dimensional Man*. Boston: Beacon Press, 1964.
Marx, Karl. *The German Ideology*. Trans. R. Pascal. New York: International, 1947.
Mumford, Lewis. *Technics and Civilization*. New York: Harcourt, Brace and World, 1934.
Nicoll, Allardyce. *Masks, Mimes and Miracles*. New York: Harcourt Brace, 1931, 1963.
Norris, Edwin, ed. and trans. *The Ancient Cornish Drama*. 2 vols. Oxford: Clarendon, 1859.
Owst, G. R. *Literature and Pulpit in Medieval England*. Cambridge: At the University Press, 1933. Rev. ed., New York: Barnes and Noble, 1961.
Pirenne, Henri. *Medieval Cities*. Princeton: Princeton University Press, 1952, 1969.
Posten, M. M. *The Medieval Economy and Society: An Economic History of Britain in the Middle Ages*. London: Weidenfeld and Nicolsen, 1972.
Power, Eileen. *The Wool Trade in English Medieval History*. Oxford: Oxford University Press, 1941.
Prosser, Eleanor. *Drama and Religion in the English Mystery Plays*. Stanford: Stanford University Press, 1961.
Rörig, Fritz. *The Medieval Town*. Berkeley and Los Angeles: University of California Press, 1969.
Rose, Martial, ed. *The Wakefield Mystery Plays*. New York: Norton, 1961.
Sastre, Alfonso. "Seven Notes on *Waiting for Godot*." Trans.

Leonard C. Pronko. Reprinted from *Primer Acto,* no. 1 (April 1957) in *Casebook on Waiting for Godot,* ed. Ruby Cohn, pp. 101–107. New York: Grove, 1967.

Serran, Genevieve. "Beckett's Clowns." In *Casebook on Waiting for Godot,* ed. Ruby Cohn. New York: Grove, 1967.

Staël-Holstein, Germaine de. *De la littérature considérée dans ses rapports avec les institutions sociales.* 2 vols. Geneva: Droz, 1959.

Stuart, Donald Clive. *The Development of Dramatic Art.* New York: Appleton, 1937.

Suvin, Darko. "Preparing for Godot—or the Purgatory of Individualism." *Tulane Drama Review (TDR)* 11, no. 4, T36 (Summer 1967): 23–36. Reprinted in *Casebook on Waiting for Godot,* ed. Cohn, pp. 121–132.

Sweedler, Carol. "American Social Melodrama, 1885–1905." Ph.D. dissertation. University of California, San Diego, 1975.

Szanto, George H. "The Dramatic Process." *Bucknell Review* 19 (Spring 1972): 3–30.

———. *Narrative Consciousness: Structure and Perception in the Fiction of Kafka, Beckett, and Robbe-Grillet.* Austin: University of Texas Press, 1972.

———. "On the Political Rhetoric of our Narrative Tastes." *Massachusetts Review* 18, no. 1 (Spring 1977): 35–50.

Taine, Hippolyte. *Essais de critique et d'histoire.* Paris: Hachette, 1887.

Weber, Max. *The Protestant Ethic and the Spirit of Capitalism.* New York: Scribner's, 1958.

Williams, Raymond. "Base and Superstructure in Marxist Cultural Theory." *New Left Review* 82 (November–December 1973): 3–16.

———. *Culture and Society, 1780 to 1950.* New York: Harper and Row, 1958.

———. *Drama from Ibsen to Eliot.* London: Chatto and Windus, 1952.

———. *Drama in Performance.* Harmondsworth, Middlesex: Penguin, 1968.

INDEX